A Most Fortunate Man

A Vietnam KIA
Pilot's Letters

A Son's Journey

This book is dedicated in memory of the other 2,207 helicopter pilots who gave their lives in Southeast Asia during the Vietnam War.

ACKNOWLEDGEMENTS-

This book would not have been possible without the unwavering belief in its importance that my wife, Laura Seeley, has shown to see I completed it. Also her mother, the late Jean C. Coffelt, was instrumental in seeing this project come to fruition.

A special note of thanks must go to Vietnam Huey helicopter pilot Doug Womack. His counsel and advice has been invaluable.

I hold a deep sense of gratitude towards the owners and staff of the BOISE WEEKLY I have worked with over the years . This paper gave me a voice when I had none and then allowed me to honor my father's writing ambition by publishing his letters three separate times.

To all of those Vietnam veterans who knew "Big John" or had a connection to his story and shared their memories I hope "thank you" will suffice. Each of you has given real meaning to the phrase...THEY ARE NOT FORGOTTEN.

Author's Note-

This book can be read in two ways. From the beginning, the top priority of this project has been to publish my father's letters-to allow him to tell his story in his words...of his experience in Vietnam. Thus, his letters are very lightly edited and his grammatical errors and miss-spellings left intact.

However, my father's story of how he earned his place on Panel 8E Line 101 of the Vietnam Wall can be learned from just reading of my journey to "find him."

To protect the privacy of the many Vietnam veterans who shared memories, I refer to them by their military titles except for those my father wrote of in his letters.

FOREWORD

As this printing goes to press the United States is in the ninth year of the conflict in Afghanistan. The national debate continues over what course to take, but the only consensus is it is not likely a war that will have a clean, simple victory… the kind of war Americans admire where we go in, kick butt, win, and come home.

Yet, this country has not had such a war since World War II. Korea was considered a stalemate where we thwarted the enemy's intention, but did not win. Vietnam was lost three years after we'd withdrawn the majority of our forces. With Vietnam we suffered our first defeat. During and after the Vietnam War the policy-makers were not reachable, but the veterans who returned were. They suffered the wrath of an angry nation. America's long hangover from Vietnam occurred as I grew up…grew up without the father my family had sacrificed early in the Vietnam War.

My father's voice went silent when I was five years old. So, for thirty years from 1966 -1996, I had no weapon to fight with. From a family that never let go of his loss I had the cursory outlines of his story-how my father loved to fly helicopters; loved his country and the United States Army that had made it possible for him to fly and he had answered the call to duty when he got his orders to go to Vietnam.

Yet, his individual actions-his honor and that of the other 58,259 who share space with him on the Wall-were confused by the American public with the war's outcome which came fully 9 years after his death. In our country's search for "peace" over its loss of over 58,000 lives, new casualties of the war were created. Home from the bullets and carnage of war the veterans of Vietnam, their families and the families of those who had given their lives found themselves defending themselves in a different kind of war.

The war that played itself out in communities across the country and in the media…movies like "Apocalypse Now" played on movie screens. It's thesis? How a deranged Colonel in Vietnam was killing his own men. Imagine such a movie with WWII as its setting? America's heroes of World War II more than likely would have picketed theaters. Anti-war protesters from Vietnam might have used again their organizing skills to protest again…this time over how their father's service could not be besmirched with a movie about a WWII Colonel killing his own soldiers. Yes, War is Hell. No one disputes that. The citizens of our country came late to the realization of how they had wronged the Vietnam veterans, but the damage has been done. The scars of the second war remain. The Vietnam Veterans of America motto: "Never again will one generation abandon another…" is so true.

So, years into another frustrating, perplexing war with no easy solution there is one clear, undisputable truth: the veterans of Iraq and Afghanistan are being treated with respect in inverse proportion to the treatment our now-aging Vietnam veterans received. Never again will returning veterans from a war suffer the blunt force trauma of our citizenry turning their back on them.

Yet, there remains those pockets of appalling insincerity and lack of appreciation for our good soldiers in Vietnam where "All gave some…some gave All". In the years of research I've put in writing this book even I've been attacked. The worst was at my local coffee shop. I was standing in line when a friend behind me said: "How is that work on that book going about your father-the helicopter pilot killed in Vietnam?"

As I turned around to answer him the thirty-something man in front of me interrupted with this: "I was a tourist in Vietnam last summer-the country your father bombed the shit out of."

I had nothing to say to this imbecile, but noted wryly how he had failed to eavesdrop close enough. This fool must not have heard the word "helicopter" for helicopters do not drop bombs.

What can be learned from the story that follows? Not much for Vietnam veterans for they know the honor they served with, but history must be told so it's not lost. My father's eloquent voice should not remain buried with him in Golden Gate National Cemetery in San Bruno, California.

CONTENTS

Chapter 1- "This Beats the Hell Out of Saigon"

Just over a month and a half before I was born the country elected John F. Kennedy as President. A few years before my birth the Soviets had won round one of the race to space with the launch of Sputnik…a nervous country awaited what this new President would say . . . how would he lead us in this new age where our Soviet adversary had bested us for the first time in the on-going Cold War that touched all of our lives.

Yet, the Seeley family was a military family so we were at "Ground Zero". Hell, I was born in a military hospital at Fort Ord, Ca. My father was serving with his first helicopter company as a Warrant Officer H-21 pilot. I was born on December 26, 1960. Just about the time John Kennedy uttered the words: "Ask not what your country can do for you, but what you can do for your country" my father was giving his answer as he left us in February 1961 for a peacetime, occupation tour in Korea…a tour extended involuntarily to 15 months from 12 months because East Germany started constructing the Berlin Wall. Just as has happened with many of our troops in Iraq now, world events kept Dad and Mom apart longer than planned. Just how taxing this separation was is born out in this 4th wedding anniversary letter my Dad wrote to Mom:

August 28, 1961

My Darling Wife,

This will be my anniversary letter to you. I am unable to find a card of any sort to carry the message. And if there were such a card available to me over here, I doubt that the words printed on it, written by some other person, could convey all that I feel in my heart. Four years now, Alice. If my memory serves me, the fourth anniversary calls for fruit and flowers.

But it seems that there is no possible way to send such a gift to you, now. And if memory still serves me, the first anniversary called for paper. Although four years have given us so much more than we could find or produce in one, thinking of you and these four years together--and the gifts of love and happiness that you have given me--I feel every bit as young and as happy as I did on our first. And so I wonder if you will accept this letter as my paper gift to you, on this day? I don't have much faith in the regularity of the U.S. mail of late, so I am writing this now, hoping that it will arrive there in time for you to read these words--on our date.

I suppose the easiest and most natural way to begin is to say very simply, "Happy anniversary." Just exactly why the word "happy" has evolved over the years, instead of some other well-suited word, I don't know. It could, just as easily have been "blessed," or "loving," or "wonderful" or any number of words. I suppose it is because happiness is such an elusive thing, we spend our entire lives in pursuit of it. Marriage seems to promise it, and in loving and needing, we wish to give that which we desire most for ourselves.

There are so many things I wish to say to you. Things I wish to mention in way of remembering, so you will know that I haven't forgotten. Things I wish to share with you, because we have shared them before. Things I wish to thank you for, because I owe so much to you--and things I wish to promise you, because promise means tomorrow.

With all of these tumbling around within me, wanting to be blurted out all at once, I'm afraid that my hand won't be able to catalogue them on paper in the manner that I desire.

I find that being in love with you--in my fashion, words of love become stumbling things--and I feel very much like a halting, nervous schoolboy. So eager to pronounce my heart, and yet afraid that I won't be able to— that I will not make the right choice of words, that I will be misunderstood, and that I will lose this chance, if I either hurry, or hesitate.

Being away from you and living from day to day upon my memories--as I must--causes certain things to come into sharp focus, and others to fade. The very nature of loneliness magnifies all of the highlights of my life with you, but not, I suspect, out of proportion, as is often the case in other matters. Dim in my memory are those small and unimportant misgivings and misunderstandings that are so common and inherent to two people living and working together toward a life of unity and happiness.

It occurs to me, that in the master scheme of life, we exist solely to love and be loved. That these are the demands and rewards of life, and that sadly, so many are caught up in the race against life, not for it, that identities and simple truths fall by the wayside. It's such a shame that this happens, as it does, all too often. If people could only remember why, and for what, they exist in the world.

Love is so often misunderstood, or never really recognized, that it is seldom thanked for what it has to give. After the first passions fade, if there is tempered a steady flame, it is the brightness of that flame that is true love. How steady it burns and how much warmth it gives and how much we are willing to give to keep it burning--these are the true measures of success of a life together.

What do I have to measure the success and happiness of my life with you in these four short years? For the present, all I have here with me are my memories, Alice. They are mine, yet I hope that some of them are yours, too. For you are responsible for all of them, my darling.

I go back to the days of our courtship, not so very long ago. I remember--as if it were yesterday--the dates we had, the telephone calls, the clothes you wore, the blue of your eyes and the realization that, while I was pursuing, I was being trapped. While I was gaining ground, I was giving ground--and what a sweet, easy surrender it seemed to be, because of you.

I remember our modest beginning. How much I wanted everything to be perfect for you, in every way. How much I owed to so many people for making it so. I remember our wedding, and its impact upon me, far beyond what I had expected. How I became suddenly aware that a life--other than my own--was now in my hands. I remember, I will never forget, how radiant you looked as you came down the aisle. How breathtaking you were on our wedding night. Our first night--and how, in the middle of that night, I awoke and leaning upon my elbow, watched you sleep and asked myself if this had really happened? And our first trip across the U.S. to a place neither of us knew anything of--not certain of our chances--but together, starting out fresh with happiness. A couple kids, remember?

I remember our first home. The first time I came home to a dinner and how you were there at the top of the stairs. How you watched every morsel of food I took that evening. And how, so many evenings, the food grew cold in the kitchen while we were busy discovering each other. How people looked at us and could tell. I remember your laughter in the dark. And those whispered words.

I remember San Francisco. Still not certain of the events to come. The apartment there, the park across the way. The way you looked as you walked down the street with the wind in your hair. My heart jumps now, Alice, remembering how my chest seemed to burst with pride at the sight of you--all woman. And I remember seeing you in maternity clothes for the first time.

I remember leaving you there in Nampa, and how the swell of your stomach seemed to tell me, "I must not fail," and how your voice over the telephone, miles away, gave me strength for another day.

And I remember that warm little home at Christmas and the night after. How I burned my tongue on coffee across the street from the hospital and how, standing there in the hall, I heard you cry out in labor and how hard I prayed. Our first child, a boy with his mother's eyes. How useless and unimportant I felt as I watched you nurse him and the serene secret that seemed to pass between the two of you.

I remember our second time in Alabama and how I drew strength from the presence of the both of you being with me.

And Salinas and Fort Ord. All of those warm, happy days watching a baby grow and finding laughter in most everything. And another child on the way.

I remember our last Christmas--how perfect it was, just as we planned it. And on a schedule that only God could plan, another boy on the next day--with his mother's eyes. I remember 30 wonderful days with Doug seeming to take over for me already, with words like, "Don't cry, Mark," and, "Dougy help," as three of us waxed the car that cold day. Remember?

And I remember standing alone over a baby crib and at the gate of the airport--saying goodbye.

Yes, Alice, I remember these and so many more things. All of this in just four short years. Memories enough to last me a lifetime. Yet I have just begun to store away these treasures, for we still have our whole lives before us. I wonder if my heart has room for any more, being so full of them now. Some of these treasures that you have given me are of everyday occurrences. Things that happen to most people, but because they have happened in my life with you, because of you, they are priceless to me, and I hold them dear in the album of my heart. I wonder what memories I have given you in return? I hope that you have as many, and that they are as wonderful as mine are to me. I have mentioned them because I can never forget. Because I wish to share them with you, and wish to thank you for them. I want to thank you, Alice, for the warmth that glows within me now--for the way you have fed this steady flame that burns and gives all of this warmth that I feel. For all of the sacrifices you have made, large and small. Dearest, I have watched you grow from girl to woman--a transition caused by the role of a wife, then mother. And yet you are still so much a girl, my girl.

I wonder if I have grown along with you, darling. Like a small boy, I have hurt you at times, if only to stir some emotion in you, to gain your attention and draw you back to me when, at times, I felt as though I was not getting my full share--needing you so--regardless of how busy or tired you may have been. Forgive me, darling.

I am afraid that I am so very basically a selfish person. So very much a small man. Yet, looking around me, I wonder if I am exclusive in this. We men are such a thin-skinned lot it seems. Always inflating ourselves with fancied and noble causes. Yet when the thin veneer of our maleness--our manhood--is stripped away, we are such little boys. And the state of the world today is because we are such children, playing in mud too deep for us. We go out and battle the odds, real and manufactured, and win against them more often than not. But we reach out for more than we can grasp, and prick ourselves on the thorns of greed and "ambition." And the bubble bursts. When this ego is deflated and we look around at our vacuum, what makes us pick ourselves up and go back for more? It is you women, I suspect. We often curse you for the complicated mechanisms that we fancy you to be, for the quiet power you wield over our lives. But without you, we would still be savages. Have we men come so very far, though? I sometimes wonder. If we could take example from women and be more genuinely concerned about our immediate responsibilities--our families instead of our ambition to outdo one another in the game we call progress--how much better off the world would be for all of us.

I look at my own person and face the truth that I see there. I don't know what or where I would be without you adding your ingredient to my life. I would still exist in this world, I imagine. But I doubt that I would be living this adventure to the full measure. Yes, I am aware of my kind of person. My flaws, my imperfections. I know that I am, like so many men, complicated and confused, self-centered and demanding, bullish and afraid. I know also what you have done to me--for me--out of a very simple and trusting love. For all of my sophisticated reasons that I conjure to exist as the person I am, you--in your clean and wholesome love--continue to clear the air in my life and provide the compass and rudder for me to set my course by.

I look at this love of ours and find that it can endure the jetsam that this world, in distress, throws up against it. It is a good love, Alice, a working marriage. It has acquired substance through the everyday practice of faith and courage, trust and sacrifice--all of that which is needed to give tone to the fiber and muscle of the strength that is required to give, and to take in this rewarding existence. Love, being the marrow of life, reaches so deep into those that are not afraid to feel it, that it can hurt, even while it ministers. Such is the case with me, being away from you now. I once read that without love, "You will laugh, but not all of your laughter, and cry, but not all of your tears." So again, I give thanks to you, Alice. Yes, for all of this loneliness and longing that I feel for you and our boys.

And in looking at our marriage, I think of our children. I realize how much they have cemented this adventure of ours. How wonderful it is-- this manner in which our lives have been enriched by their presence-- and the new and ever-changing formulas they offer to the chemistry of our love. How can I tell you how much they mean to me? They mean so very much, Alice. Far more than innocent objects of love, they are the third dimension--the flesh, to all my hopes and prayers for a better world.

I look at these four years with you and wonder what I can promise you in return for all of this? Would the vows that I took in marriage, four short years ago, be enough? If so, I promise now, all that those vows--both silent and spoken--promised you then. I promise you--everything. Yet I know that I shall fail from time to time. So I promise that I shall keep on trying, a little harder each time, to measure up to all of the faith that you have in me. Until I can return and show you with actions, all this that I promise you, these written words will have to suffice. Please accept them then, my darling, for they are all I have to offer you now, so very far away.

I will return to my family and resume living there--in that other world, with a renewed dedication--out of a thankfulness for all that I have been given. But for now, in these alien surroundings, so void of the familiar sights and sounds that represent the life that we have made together. I am sustained by such gentle, quiet visions. They speak out to me now, across the miles that separate us.

A bed, with two pillows side-by-side; a tired, bedraggled, stuffed toy duck; the clutter of toys on the floor and the scent of baby talcum in the air.

So for all of the happiness that you have given me, for everything that has been, is now, and will be, I say that "I love you."

And thank you, Princess

Happy Anniversary

From your husband,

John

Just as with his 55 letters home from Vietnam before he was killed on June 27, 1966 my father left a written legacy of his service in Korea. It was actually his second time in Korea for as a young man my father had been in the Army to fulfill his required obligation to serve. In his service from 1952-54 Dad was a military policeman-an MP. It was not a job he liked at all. As you will see in his letters he was a personable and sensitive man...but at 6' 4" tall he felt others thought, as a military policeman, he used his size to intimidate others.

Once he completed his compulsory military service Dad returned to the city he was born and raised in. He went to Pasadena City College, but from his records I obtained his grades were declining by his 3rd semester. He announced to his old high school buddy who had introduced him to my mother that he was going back into the Army and he was going for choppers. His friend, already married with children, had also done his compulsory military service and come home to Pasadena. His friend, Chuck Frady, was punching a ten-key at the auto dealership my Mother had found a job at.

Mom had graduated from high school in Idaho determined to escape from becoming a farmer's wife. She had seen enough of her father's struggle as a poor farmer. Unable to afford a car, she piled into a girlfriend's car. They took their typing skills to the promise of California. Within months Chuck Frady arranged a date for his co-worker with his old high school buddy-my Dad.

So when Dad announced his was aiming to go join the Army again with the goal of applying for flight school his friend thought "I'm not letting John go off and have all the fun." Dad had left the Army as an E-3 or E-4 in 1954. Yet, he went back in as a Private and went through boot camp again. Dad reasoned he could get an assignment to a helicopter company and from there apply for flight school.

Once he and Chuck Frady were in boot camp they became fast friends with another trainee who aspired to become a pilot as well. Their fates became intertwined then. Ultimately this new friend-Ron Rodgers-became a pilot as well. After his own tour in Korea Ron had little time at home before he was sent to Vietnam in 1962 ...just as Dad wrote home happened to many pilots. After his Vietnam tour Ron had met his obligation and got out of the Army. He spent the Vietnam War under civilian contract as a helicopter pilot instructor at Camp Wolters in Texas. Then, he went on in the 1970's to adopt the Lifeflight concept to the half of the state of Nebraska he settled in.

As you will read Father was not at all happy to be separated from his family, but he liked Korea and the Korean people. Once he arrived he looked up a Korean woman he had known from his first tour years earlier. The woman wrote to her old friend's wife the following letter:

August 14, 1961

Dear Mrs. Seeley:

How are you in these hot days Mrs. Seeley? And also how is Douglas doing?

One day morning of May, John suddenly appeared to me in my office. So great joy and happiness was for both John and I. After nearly 7 years of absence we finally meet again. It is very nice to have him again in Korea.

My family are also very well. As you may know, I have two daughters one is five years old (4 years old in American age) and the other is 4 years old (3 years in American age). I am expecting to have one more baby in September this year. I hope to have a boy this time as I already get plenty of girls.

Perhaps you can not understand me why I favor boy. However, it is long traditional custom in Orient. People in Orient always favored boy rather than girl. Though this thinking is changing nowadays quite a degree of the custom is still existing in Korea.

Mr. Seeley is always thinking of his fine family, you and his sons. I found good husband, good father and fortitude in him.

John is always doing his best to build himself. Really I am fortunate to have him in Korea once again. God always be with him, and send him to you in good health. I will write you again,

Truly yours,
Kim, Dong Sung

My grandfather died in 1984, but never really recovered from his son's death. Yet, that love led him to preserve and save much that made this book possible. Without him the letters from Korea and Fort Belvoir that follow here would be lost forever. Inside the pine box he built that held his son's medals he had saved in a sandwich bag seven letters Dad wrote to him. Here is some of what my father wrote from Korea beside his beautiful 4th wedding anniversary letter:

Saturday, Oct. 21, 1961

Dear Family-

Well here we are out in the boondocks. The whole company moved up here two days ago and we are living in tents. The purpose behind all of this is to provide immediate support to the Republic of Korea Army in their full maneuvers. Living out here isn't bad-we have diesel stoves in the tents and folding cots to sleep on. Sure as hell-it rained the first days and everything is covered with mud. We are in the valley that appears to be prone to fog since it hangs in here just about every morning. If did not yesterday and we got up at 4:00 AM to fly a 10 ship mission hauling troops to the attack area. You should smell the inside of an H-21 after a bunch of Koreans have been inside. Wow! I was the second ship in the flight and managed to hang rather close to the flight leader who had the best ship (of course) and went hell-bent for election. But on the 4th haul on take-off I got caught in his rotor downwash and already had the engine red-lined because of the load. There was nothing I could do but hang on and see what happened. I settled back down and the gear struck a few times before I bounced up again. By then I was at about 60 knots and over the river bank.

So it was either total an aircraft or burn up an engine- so I wrapped in power and managed to keep flying long enough to make a 'go-around' and land. So now my aircraft is on the ground for an engine change and I won't be flying for a few days-nothing to do but sit and twiddle my thumbs. Living out here reminds me of seven years ago and I wonder what has become of all my old tent mates? If I had my choice I would take them as companions any day.

Well, folks I don't know why I wrote this-had nothing to say really-just using up time. I wrote Carol, {his step-sister. His mother died of a premature heart attack when Dad was 24 and his Dad had remarried a widowed woman named Ruth who had brought a daughter to the marriage} *at the address you sent to me Ruth-hope they are making out O.K.*

I'm taking some pictures out here too and when they are developed-will send you some snaps.
Love-John

During my father's time with the 6th Transportation Company their base was known as Camp K-6. The base is still in operation today, but is known as Camp Humphreys. Dad's next letter to my grandfather holds the answer to why the name of the base was changed.

Thurs. Nov. 16, 1961
Dear Dad-
Weeks ago I made a mark on my Calendar, noting this day as your birthday and intended to purchase a card to send to you. It seems as this was only yesterday. Where the last few weeks have gone I do not know.

So, I apoligize for not having sent a remembrance to arrive there in time. Letting you know that I remember. Happy Birthday Father

Time has fled these last few weeks or at since we have come in from the field. I am still swamped in my job as Post Billeting officer and I usually fall asleep at 7:00 PM anymore. It helps the time rush by.

I have been informed that I am next to take our aircraft to Japan for rebuilding but don't know when I will leave since all H-21's are grounded worldwide.

I suppose you have seen or heard the news back there of 'our accident' over here. It happened Monday. A few ships had early morning take-offs that day and night after briefing we were notified by the Air Force at Osan (just north of here) that one of our a/c [aircraft] was seen laying in two pieces west of their field about 3 miles

We dispatched some ships right away but no good was done since there were no survivors.

All that is known now, is that it was observed at 300 feet turning end over end then splitting into two pieces.

One of our best first pilots CWO Ben Humphreys was at the controls with a Capt. as a Co-Pilot. I knew the crew chief from Fort Ord days. A total of 7 people were killed.

The services were held yesterday and many people-friends of Ben's came from all over-by jeep, all night traveling to be here.

Now the experts are here from the U.S. and Japan to find out what happened. So, there will be no flying for quite awhile yet. Not much else to write-except my love and regards to all. And Happy Birthday

> *Love,*
> *John*

As is so often the case with soldiers stationed far from loved ones, it does not take the drama of almost losing control of his ship or news of an accident to prompt letters home. The mundane becomes important. As witnessed by the following letter that has little of dramatic or historical note, it still provides a fuller picture of John Seeley's experience in Korea.

December 1, 1961

Dear Family:

....I had returned from Japan the night before and am now getting caught up on things. As far as the trip to Japan goes-it was pleasant to get away from this hole for a while. Japan impressed me greatly in respect of money and how much they have over there. The prices are higher than for most goods than they are in the States for like items. No bargains to speak of except on junk...

We were gone for 8 days altogether. I can't say I had a good time-I didn't try. I just walked the streets and rode the streetcars and looked in the dept. stores and etc.

We flew a ship over for repair and brought a revamped one back. That's about all there is to say for the whole trip. Back here things are normal-the C.O. hasn't cracked up yet but I am sure he is on the verge of it. Everybody is totally disgusted.

News has it that two chopper units left the States for Saigon. Another one to Alaska- another to Hawaii and two more getting ready to go to the Far East. Many men who had just returned from Korea are in the units that left for Saigon. Some only had 60 days back in the States. There is hardly a Unit left there to return to when I leave here. If I could find a way to earn a living outside the Army now-I would tell them to shove it! They knew 2-3 years ago where Units were needed but Wash. wouldn't send them so now everybody's assignment picture is all fouled up. My time with my family means more than anything and this B.S is too much.

I did make what I consider to be a wise investment. I bought two battery-powered tape recorders ($17.00 each) I will send one to my Alice for X-MAS and we can correspond on tape rather than by pen. It will be a pleasant surprise for them-I hope, but I know my morale will be lifted-hearing their voices once again...

Well 201 days gone and 181 to go unless they continue with the 90 day extension which would make it 271 to go.

That's about all the news from over in this puke-hole. Nothing really worth writing about. My love to all back there and I hope the new address turns out to be a very pleasant experience.

Take care all
LOVE,
John

Then in a letter to very close friends of his father Dad gave a great overview of his duties...

Jan, 9, 1962

Dear Elmo and Imo-

I took down my Xmas Cards this evening and made a note of the people I have neglected to write to since I have been over here.

There isn't much to write about my life here since it is not interesting to me and all of the news is being generated elsewhere in the world these days.

I am stationed with one of two Cargo chopper units that are in Korea. Ours being located 60 miles south of Seoul near the Yellow Sea. From here we fly to just about all sections of Korea providing support for the both the U.S. and the Korean Armies. About 50% of the missions are VIP hauls which are a supreme pain. Once in awhile we get missions that pose a real challenge and are interesting enough to remember. Dec. 26, I flew Korea's head hatchet man-General Park to various observation posts along the truce line where he handed out bottles of Scotch to his top 'yes-men'-see what I mean? The only real kicks on that job was thumbing my nose out the window at the Field Glasses that I knew were watching us 2000 meters away, on the 'bad guys' side. But I shouldn't complain,-all of it counts off the tour and I would be stir crazy if I couldn't fly and get away from the things and people who drive me nuts.

But that is true no matter where I am. For a few hours out of the day I can escape into another world and come back with a new perspective on things..

Korea happens to be a very beautiful sight from the air-plenty of contrast, especially in the spring and summer-and flying here is rewarding considering the panorama one is afforded. The winter months and lousy weather knock our flying time down quite a bit and so most of the guys go in the deep freeze at the bar or in the sack a little earlier than usual. I spend my time on an additional duty-Post Billeting Officer, which is a bag of worms but provides me with the best set of quarters on post equal to the Colonel's. So with a place to hang my hat as nice as this-I seldom go out-even to a movie-anymore.

I spend my time writing Alice-or reading books-and sleeping until I get bedsores...
I hope to come home in early June but may not make it until September. In the meantime, this beats the hell out of Saigon where a lot of my buddies are. That's about it from here folks-thanks for the newsy Xmas card-take care and stay healthy.
See you-or write you soon.
Love
John

Perhaps, these VIP flights led to his next assignment. After gaining a National Security Clearance Dad was assigned to the 3rd. Transportation Corps at Fort Belvoir, Virginia. His job there required him to fly many VIP hauls, but their mission they trained constantly for was to evacuate the nation's leaders in the event nuclear war broke out. We were at Fort Belvoir from late 1962 through part of 1964.

Of course, I was too young to remember any of this, but one letter exists that shows Dad's awareness of his impending date with Vietnam and how he drank in the experience of being a young father while he still had time. In a letter to his Dad dated August 7 of 1963 he included this...

Lately-I have missed you so much. Doug and Mark are responsible for this feeling. God, I wish you could see and hear them now. Doug is huge! And a couple of days ago he jumped off the low board in the swimming pool into the deep end because he trusted me. I was treading water and told him I would get him as soon as he jumped. The little guy was scared stiff but did it anyway. He can dive in the shallow end and sort of tadpole swim about 10 feet before he has to put his foot down. He is as large as kids 6 or 7 around here and I have to catch myself many times and remember he is only 4 1/2 and needs that kind of attention. Mark dotes on me a lot now and announces to the whole neighborhood that I am home from work. He is the stubborn one of the two and has an iron will. Sort of reminds me of Sis...

Ironically, the one station where memories of my father are most vivid, there are no letters. John S. Seeley accepted a direct commission from Warrant Officer to 1st Lieutenant and "North to Alaska" we went. That treasured time-from mid '64 to mid '65 was all too brief for all of us...given what was to happen.

Father jockeyed for assignments at home-not wanting to leave us. Yet, Lyndon Johnson committed the United States fully to the conflict in Vietnam in 1965. Faced with the stark reality of the cruel vicissitudes of war father wrote to extended family a letter of his wishes in the event he did not return.

November 7, '65
Columbus, Ga.

Dear Family:

I cannot recall when the last letter was sent to you from us-but no matter when it was, a lot has happened. I do know that we telephoned you while at Disneyland-but no answer. I guess the family was on vacation in B.C. as Cynthia had advised us.

So to fill you in from the beginning which was early July:

We had planned a nice 30 day vacation in Alaska, starting in late July. Yet the Viet-Nam mess caught up with us and damned near every pilot in the outfit got orders to the U.S. for further overseas shipment. Leaving our home up there was rough all around and the ensuing move was a blast.

The VW blew up in Terrace B.C. after we left the ferry-so another used engine got us to Seattle where I bought us a new Buick. Then on to Calif. to see the folks and Sis for awhile before Southern Calif. and Disneyland. At that time, the last word I had from 'sources'-was at least 30 days at Ft. Benning-at the most 60 days. So I pulled out all the stops and tried to buy out Disneyland. The kids had a ball-all four of them.

Then on to Benning. What a place! The 1st Cav. had just left for Viet-Nam and the place was in an uproar. I reported in on 1 Sept. with over 250 aviators from around the world. Everyone in the same situation or worse: Family one place, furniture another place etc. Alice and the kids were with me by a fluke of luck and indecision-we couldn't decide on a home in Calif. and she finally decided she was coming along-no matter what.

We have rented a nice apartment-Doug is in a fine school (1st grade) and doing well. We're broke and happy for the time being-counting the days. Most of my unit from Alaska went into UH-1B helicopters and have departed for Viet-Nam. I was high man in tandem rotor time, so I was held back to form a new CH-47 'Chinook' outfit. I know all of this military yak is of little interest to you-but after years in the old H-21, I was overjoyed to be selected for its big brother instead of going into one of those kamikaze outfits. Now the powers are turning a beautiful bird like the Chinook into a damned B-17. Anyway-the C.O. and I have policed up a lot of talented people-many old friends and we have a unit of good, stable talent.

Without violating any security-I can tell you that I expect to be out of here by Feb. Alice will likely go back to California-Sacramento area we think-its still up in the air. In the meantime we are tying up loose ends on the family affairs and that is what prompted this letter.

In reviewing my personal affairs-I have stated in my will that I want my Step-sister, Carol and her husband to take care of Doug and Mark in the event Alice should not survive me. Because of Cynthia's plans and etc. we think this would be better all the way around. If the finger should point to me and Alice is widowed, she will have $43,000 Life Insurance plus Social Security and Widows benefits from the Army. We are still in the process of determining the breakdown on Insurance etc. over the remaining years. In this respect-$20,000 would go for either a home or investments until such time as she would want a home.

Lee, I have nobody else in my mind except you as regards to advice to Alice on how to invest and etc. and I wonder if your services would be available if such should be the case?

Please let me know your thoughts on this and any mechanics of the deal that I should negotiate in a revised will-if the answer is in the affirmative. Things are getting down to the line now and before I leave I would like to hand her a packaged sense of security. So your response is awaited...

Regards to all,
John

Unfortunately, all my father planned for happened.

He did move us back out to California and he sailed away to Vietnam on February 26, 1966.

On June 27, 1966 the CH-47 he was co-piloting in Vietnam crashed…sending his wife and two boys into the life all military families know the ultimate sacrifice might require.

18

Chapter 2: The Years Without

The medals ceremony was the final curtain to John Seeley's military career. My grandfather's friend noted: "The ceremony and medals will impress upon the boys the greatness of what their father did for his country, but I believe soldiers should be recognized for what they do while they are alive."

Life, of course, had to go on. In my five year old innocence, I continued to smile, laugh, explore, and learn. Later, the innocence of a little boy would give way to the layered, multiple questions of pending puberty. My dead father was lost, but to somewhere good and safe-no more war, Mommy had told me so. In my child's mind I willed this belief because good Daddies go to good places.

My mother did not allow my brother and I to attend my father's burial with 21 gun salute at Golden Gate National Cemetery. When my 57 year old step-father widowed my mother a second time Mom was 51. On a visit back to Boise after his death I found a book on grieving Mom had bought. In a chapter on children and death it said: " It is fundamental no matter the age of the child that the child go to the funeral; see the dirt go on the casket; and see it lowered into the Earth so the child knows the finality of death." Fatal to any hope of 'letting go' was another passage: the trauma triangle is at its lowest level at age three for there is no substantial memory of the dead and then the triangle reaches its apex at age five for a five year-old has memories of the dead, but no concept that death is lasting and final. At age seven death's finality is understood and the trauma is level and as consequential to the seven year old as the three year old except the seven year old, my brother's age, carries the weight of more memories.

When I read this passage in that book on grieving in 1989 things began to make sense. No wonder the memory of our final goodbye had stayed with me piercing my mind and heart through the years like an unwelcome thief...robbing me suddenly of whatever good I had in the moments when that hug goodbye would grab me. Absent at his funeral my last memory was of life...of that goodbye. And then-since I never saw the dirt go on the casket or have someone explain at the funeral: "OK, Mark. Your Daddy is in that box, it's called a coffin."

Mom-always a wise steward of money-moved us from that big house. From the backyard with the creek that you will read so worried Dad over in Vietnam; from where Doug and I played "Bud" and "Sir" with our Gemini space capsule; from where it all crashed when the two officers showed up that fateful morning Mom opened the door and said: "Oh My God. Is he wounded?" Their silence and request to step inside was that moment of terrifying clarity. Years later I recall her telling me how slowly she made the coffee water they requested. If only she didn't step back into that living room with the Notification Officer and Chaplain then she couldn't be told what she already knew...she was now a very alone widow.

I slept that morning away while my brother heard my mother crying and knew. We spent that day over at my step-aunt's house. We swam in their pool...me just a five year old just loving being in the aunt's big pool. For my brother it was not at all a 7 year-old at play. He looked across the huge lawn my step-Uncle, a United Airlines pilot and former Navy carrier Aviator, had at this house that had been passed down through three generations. The crying Doug heard continued, but now it was my mother and step-aunt with my step-uncle fulfilling the stoic and strong male role well and admirably.

We returned to the Army Lieutenant-promoted-to-Captain home that evening.

My only memory was sitting on the edge of my older brother's bed with him. We were told and I ran over and swan-dived on my bed crying only as a child can when they find out their Daddy or Mommy is dead. Yet, I remember looking over to what I thought was my brother looking up in shock at my mother. Thirty one years later I would find out that wasn't at all why he was looking up at Mom. Actually, my brother had heard my mother crying that morning and realized what must have happened. Mom could not get the words out that he was dead. I asked if he was wounded and my brother shouted: "No Mark, he's dead." That was when I made the swan-dive on to my bed. My brother was actually asking if dad had received cookies we had baked and mailed to him. Mom had no answer for him until she received Dad's final letter days after she knew he was dead. In the letter's opening paragraph Dad wrote: "*I opened the box and ate some of the cookies as I read your first two letters*"

In the protection of a five year old's simple world I was not to learn of the extent, the depth of the emotional devastation that her husband's death had caused my mother until after I was shown the letters excerpted in this book...and that is to Alice Seeley's credit. She made miss-steps like refusing the idea of counseling for the "Seeley" boys over their father's death and not allowing us to go to his burial. Yet these mistakes are understandable. Not only did we live away from the support of a military base with couples that would have extended the sympathy only military families know how to offer in such a time, but there were no "Dr. Phil" pop psychology shows to guide my mother in the confusion of her grief over what to do with those two little boys with no Daddy at the helm to direct our destiny.

Yet probably as a result of this I had the same dream...over and over. Though we had moved to a small apartment, the dream was always in that big house.

I would hear the door bell ring. In my pajamas I would get out of bed, go down the three steps and turn right. The front door had a dividing wall behind it. Once you walked around that wall, there was a fireplace on the wall's opposite side and the living room area. Anyway, in the recurring dream I'd open the door and look way up, see my 6' 4" father, and say: "Daddy, you're home!" The sky was always so bright behind him as to almost be blinding. Years later when the final good-bye would haunt and heartbreak me, I thought of the irony of the fact the day we hugged goodbye the sky behind him was overcast-and sad. I'm certain the reason it was almost impossible to see him is because the sun's brightness was- in my dream as a five to six year old- a metaphor for hope.

Other than his medal ceremony between the age of 5 and 11 only two memories stood out. The first was the day I showed my father's medals for show-and-tell at school. It is not an experience I ever repeated. I stood up and explained each medal: The Distinguished Flying Cross; the Bronze Star; the Air Medal; and the Vietnamese Cross of Gallantry with Palm Leaf. I only said my Daddy had been killed when his helicopter crashed.

Afterwards, at recess, kids ran up to me surrounding me in a half-circle like eager beavers all asking if my father had been shot down, It seemed almost like they were asking about a cartoon. I just didn't want to answer them. I wanted to scream at them: "This was real...it wasn't a cartoon." The medals were returned to Grandad to be put back in the pine box Grandad had special made to hold his only son's things . . . a pine box whose opening in 1997 was to transform my life.

The other was a family visit to him...to Golden Gate National Cemetery in San Bruno, Ca.-south of San Francisco on the Peninsula. I was 9 or 10 at the time. Did we take one or two cars? I don't remember. I do recall the trip there included my grandfather, grandmother, and my step-aunt. Despite the passage of five or six years no stop at graves registration was needed. Dad rested on a slight slope on the side of the cemetery closest to the ocean. I liked that.

Yet, I had not reached the age of really feeling the loss of him; so this visit was etched in my memory, but carried no profound sorrow. For my mother and grandfather and step-aunt this was, of course, an extremely difficult moment. Tears were shed and the talk among the adults muted and sorrow-filled. Had this visit taken place just a few years later the toll on me would have been profoundly different. For when I was about twelve I went through a stage of mourning that was intense and often.

Every few weeks I would close the door to my room and wet my pillow with my tears...looking at a favorite photo of him and crying. There he was with his trademark confident grin looking out of an H-21 helicopter. I had been told this photo was taken when my father had served a peacetime tour in Korea. The memory of that final hug goodbye would pierce its way through my weakened defenses and leave me sobbing uncontrollably.

One session was interrupted by a knock at my door. It was my mother. "Son, can I come in for a minute?" she asked plaintively.

"No, go away!" I demanded. I did not want my mother to see her 12 year old boy weeping.

"Please Mark…I just want to tell you something and I'll leave right away. I promise," she pleaded.

"OK," I yielded.

I did not look up: my face determinedly buried in my pillow. She sat on the edge of the bed next to my left hip.

Then, in the space of a minute or so, she gave me one of the greatest gifts of my childhood. Had she told me it was OK with Mommy that I weep over the loss of this father than I would have gutted up from that point forward, but instead she said: "I don't have to tell you your father was every inch a man, but I want you to know something about your dad. Because he was a soldier you might not think your dad was this way, but he was. He never felt it unmanly to show emotion…to cry as you are now son. He believed if a man was afraid to show emotion …to cry…than he must doubt he is a man. Your father knew he was a man and crying was just being human. That's all son. I just wanted you to know this about your dad." She got up and left.

Dad cried! I'd seen his tears that last time, that last goodbye, but in my 12 year old mind that had been an exception. From those few words that day I never again felt shame over these crying sessions I went through for nearly a year; never again when a hammer of life's sorrows- a family death; some adolescent reversal; some huge set back in adulthood…some moment where tears are the natural response of a human-never again did the admonition: "Real men don't cry" ever whisper its condemnation to me.

Looking back, I think my grandfather fed this pubescent sorrow. At around the age of 11 my grandfather-who Mom, Doug, and I visited at least three times a year-began to usher my brother and I into his den to hear stories about his son…a son who I learned later he had a very tortured relationship with, but his death had washed away all of that. So, we heard military stories of what our father had done for his country, not only in Vietnam, but before that. He'd been challenged and won a knock-down drag-out fight in some training when, because of Dad's 6'4" stature, he was challenged 'king-of-the-hill' fashion. Then, there were those stories too fantastic for me to believe. One story was how "your father was at Andrews the night of JFK's assassination and Robert Kennedy, Taylor, and McNamara walked by him to meet Air Force One with LBJ, Jackie, and the slain President's body."

I recall asking Mom if this was true. "Son, it rings a vague bell, but I can't tell you for sure."

More than a few times Grandad's stories about our father would come to an abrupt halt. Grandad would suddenly break down and start sobbing. My brother and I would look at each other and know it was "tip-toe time." We would get up from our yoga-like crouches at the foot of his chair and quietly walk out without a word leaving Grandfather alone in his den. There were times he cried so hard his body shook in his chair.

Grandfather and my step-grandmother (Always Grandma to me since my grandmother had died prematurely of heart attack almost four years before I was born) lived up the freeway-I-80-in both Grass Valley and then Nevada City. When I was 11 finally there was a place where Grandad could go to visit his boy. The year was 1971. The war was still going on when the residents of these neighboring cities decided to honor the sacrifice of their local boys in this unpopular war. Plaques were bronzed and placed on the freeway overpasses. Dad had been raised in Pasadena with my aunt Cynthia. He had never lived in either city, but when Grandad got wind of these proposed memorials he asked if his "boy" could be memorialized with a plaque for the life Dad had given five years earlier. His wish was granted and, as far as I know, this plaque is still on Gold Flat Rd. overpass on Highway 49.

A special ceremony was held in some old wooden building so common to this former Gold Rush town. Of course, there was special seating in the front rows for the families. It was held during that emotionally vulnerable stage for me. I was the only family member to get up and leave…walking down the center aisle with people looking at me crying as I walked by them trying to reach the fresh foothills-of-the-Sierra mountain range air and away from my suffocating sorrow.

Then, an idea as I sat idly at my fifth grade desk one day. "What about a newspaper of Seeley family happenings? No, that wouldn't interest anyone. What about a school newspaper?" Thus, a diversion from my sorrow was created. The SEELEY TRIBUNE was born. My newspaper had a Feature Story, a Power Person of the Week (I can proudly say I was ahead of Time Inc.'s "PEOPLE" magazine with this celebrity profile marketing technique. I knew if I profiled one student than that person's friends would buy that issue) and a Sports section and Ads section. I would type up my weekly issue on "8 1/2 by 11" paper and run off copies in the school's office. The paper became popular. I tried to write to the comprehension of my readers with feature stories on a ski trip or the time a hot-air balloon landed in the huge open, undeveloped space behind the home Mom had bought. In a neighborhood of young families this starter home was what Mom could afford after the first marriage to my step-dad had dissolved and our short one-and-a-half years in a house on a golf course had ended. Yet, my first issue for 6th grade I opened with an explanation that President Nixon's lifting of price controls had forced me to raise my single-issue price from 3 cents to 5 cents.

Then, in the Spring of my 6th grade year the President of the League heard about my journalistic endeavor and approached my mother with an idea: "How about your son writing a Little League newspaper?" Issues would be free and I would be paid the princely sum of $12 a week. Ultimately, I was to be the scribe for the TRI CITY SCOOP for four years. The first year brought me a heady measure of local acclaim with articles on my newspapers written about in three local weekly newspapers and a paragraph in a columnist for the SACRAMENTO BEE that started with "The City of Rocklin is proud of 12 year old Mark Seeley's…"

One day I went out to get our mail and a letter with my name, then editor of SEELEY TRIBUNE and TRI-CITY SCOOP as the only entry on the address line, and Rocklin, Ca. on third line was in my hand. The letter was from Hollywood. A screenwriter for the CAROL BURNETT SHOW and ALL IN THE FAMILY wrote me explaining he had written a block newspaper he sold to neighbors as a kid and wanted to encourage my efforts. He enclosed a $5 check requesting an ad that said: "Dear Mark: The pen is mightier than the sword." Not wanting to look a gift horse in the mouth, I wrote back and this screenwriter attempted to be my mentor. Our correspondence continued through my freshman year in college.

He ended our correspondence after I wrote to tell him I was stopping work again on a manuscript he felt held promise. He wrote: "You squander a talent few have. Our friendship is over."

My mother was struck down with breast cancer when I was 15. My brother was not living at home; my Dad was dead; and I buckled. From a son who took my mother out each Mother's Day to the finest restaurant I could afford, I became a seriously delinquent teen for six months shouting: "Bitch, get out of my room. I'm not going to school." The concept of 'tough love' had not gelled yet. So-for a six-month period that remains a black hole-I was allowed to find my own way back to sanity. Filled with remorse over my behavior I tried to make good. Yet, my truancy had led to being sent to the school district's alternative school-"Adelante." I became the correspondent to the local ROSEVILLE PRESS TRIBUNE and we started an outreach program to change the image of the school in the communities of Rocklin and Roseville the school served. With my writing talent and public speaking ability we showed our slide show of Adelante to local philanthropic, social organizations like Rotary and Soroptimists. I was the main speaker. I was a big fish in a little pond.

Then, my mother asked my step-father if they could try again. He was leaving the state to take a computer programmer job and Mom wanted to get together with him again. I was the only of the 4 children under the age of 18. My race to get back in Mom's good graces had run out of time. They reunited and we moved to Boise, Idaho.

Mom had been raised during her high school years in Boise's neighboring town of Nampa-it's where her step-mother still lived. For her it was ideal.

So, when my step-dad accepted Mom's plea they try again the location where Ken had accepted this new job was for Mom a real homecoming. For me it was Hell. In the crazy looseness of the 1970's I was suddenly looking out from the designated smoking area at Meridian High School at a vacant field where minors who couldn't legally buy tobacco could smoke. From growing up in one town since dad's death to this? I was a faceless, new student in a big high school. To Mom it was my 'second' chance at a traditional high school. To me I'd been moved to a miserable oblivion.

So, I intentionally missed too many days of school and was expelled. I became an emancipated minor and at age 17 I used the $2,200 value of a $5,000 mutual fund Mom had gotten for me from her $35,000 death benefit when John Seeley was killed and I bought a Dodge Charger to re-start my life back where I'd grown-up. Yet, the 'outreach program' at Adelante had collapsed. So, I dropped out of high school and started college with the G.I. Bill my dad's death had left me. I only went one semester at Sierra Junior College before returning to Idaho, obtaining a GED, and resuming my education at Boise State University. I graduated in 1984 with a B.A. in Political Science after switching from my original major of journalism. Yet, one seminal event concerning Dad occurred while I was still living back down in California in 1978-'79. I paid my first solo visit to Dad's gravesite.

Free and 'emancipated' at the age of 17 was a good feeling. After the decision to drop out of high school and start college at the junior college, I began to receive monthly payments from the Veterans Administration. My dead father was making this all possible. Was it out of a sense of obligation or longing? I cannot remember now. Yet, it gnawed at me: the need to go down to San Bruno...visit that gravesite...pay my respects.

I had always kind of marched to my own drummer with my SEELEY TRIBUNE and TRI-CITY SCOOP. A lot of my free time was consumed hanging out at the local Denny's. I preferred the conversation and company of my elders more than my peers; combine that with cigarettes and a voracious appetite for coffee and there was only one place where I'd spend my free time outside of my textbooks: Denny's restaurant. In the late 1970's the veterans of WWII were in their fifties. I can recall listening in rapture to the stories of combat of those willing to talk about it.

Yet, I was at my local Denny's in Roseville, Ca. around two in the morning one night. Two hitchhikers asked me if I was on a break from some long trek on Interstate 80 adjacent to the restaurant. I told them no, but asked where they were trying to get to.

"San Francisco," one answered.

I nodded an acknowledgement and then thought hard for a few minutes and responded: "Ah, hell, I'm pumped up on three hours of coffee. I'll drop you off in S.F. because I need to go south of there and do something I've needed to do."

I have to laugh at the recollection of that because I did drop them off at some freeway juncture and then drove into San Francisco proper looking for somewhere to eat. It was about six-thirty a.m. and I think it was a weekend or holiday. So, I pulled into the parking lot of the first diner I saw. Not one woman was in that restaurant, but I'd already ordered my breakfast when the male cook came from the cook's line out to get a beverage. He had a bouffant-hairdo '60's Jackie Kennedy style. I knew I was in San Francisco!

Golden Gate National Cemetery sits on a huge plot of land between the freeway and the ocean. Some homes serve as a buffer on lower ground that separate the cemetery from the ocean. So, it affords a beautiful view of the ocean.

As I drove in, the sheer size of the cemetery struck me. Yet I still thought memory would be adequate to the task. I knew my father was past a tree toward the ocean side on a slope. Yet, small roads wound through this huge expanse endlessly. The entrance to the cemetery and its hallowed ground was at a high point. The roads stretched out like vessels to the heart reaching out to all its parts: thousands upon thousands of headstones in precise order and the exact same size. The military may be a rigid caste system of officers and enlisted, but there is no rank in death. Those who had lived out the full measure of their lives to die of old age are neighbors of those who had given the fullest measure in the flower of their youth.

I drove slowly to where my memory of eight years earlier told me to go. Foolish, I guess, but I thought even if my memory failed me, instinct and love would take to my father's headstone. I stopped by a tree that answered memory's call, but he was not there.

I returned to my car and drove back up to a building that had a sign: 'Graves Registration.' It was closed. I was crestfallen.

Since that frenetic visit at 10 I'd come too far through the pubescent sorrow stage at 12; living through the fall of Saigon in 1975; through the venom surfacing in the mid-late 70's about the veterans who'd "lost" Vietnam; the vitriol Californians often spread with statements like: "These damn Vietnamese boat people moving here and living fifteen people to an apartment like rats." No, damn it, I am going find Dad, I told myself.

I drove my car back down through the vessels-through the roads-and made many stops near trees facing the ocean side on a slight slope. As my search seemed to be failing I thought to myself: "God knows, I had failed this father of mine; failed his widow after she went under the surgeon's knife; failed to finish high school. I couldn't fail this." I stopped looking at my watch or counting the stops so as not to be further discouraged.

I'm certain my search had lasted over three hours. As I looked at headstone after headstone, I took note of the ones whose lives had been cut short…so many made Dad's death at 34 look like a blessing. I recalled what my mother had said one time when I'd asked her how she got through the funeral she did not allow my brother and I to attend.

"Mark, when we pulled into that huge cemetery I saw all the headstones and thought: "You can get through this Alice...you are not-by far-the first war widow. That gave me strength."

Suddenly, there he was

JOHN S. SEELEY
U.S. ARMY
APRIL 10 1932
JUNE 27 1966
KOREA
VIETNAM

Strangely, at the spot I thought I would be most likely to cry-I did not. Kneeling down I looked at the headstone and then thought of how close this burial plot was to the Peninsula ocean; knowing we had hugged him goodbye in February 1966 and that he had sailed away somewhere out on that very same body of water so very long ago.

Can I say he had come home to a beautiful spot? For that is what I thought. I made some apologies to him and some promises. I didn't want to leave him after this three hour trek past hundreds and hundreds of headstones. Just as he had to leave us some twelve years earlier because his country called him to do so…I had to leave, but for a much simpler and far less noble reason. I had a life to go on with…without him. I kissed my hand to his headstone, drew a deep breath and bolted up. I walked quickly to my car. I could feel love's tug pulling me back, but I had to go on.

CHAPTER 3: "Footprints in the Snow..."

Following that 1979 visit to his grave-site I guess it could be said my life proceeded in un-distinguished fashion. Yes, I went on to college and graduated with a degree in Political Science in 1984. Anytime, I told anyone of this achievement I gave my father credit. His G.I. bill made my education possible.

Yet, I did little with the education I had gotten. I proposed to a college girlfriend, but broke off the engagement after resigning from a "career-starting" job.

Within a few months of graduation I had landed a job as field representative for a non-profit company. I did community organizing and fund-raising for a non-profit: the March of Dimes. I was based out of Boise, Idaho but it was a two hour drive to the southern-most of my 12 counties in northern Idaho. I loved the job, but hated the constant travel. I resigned in less than a year and became what I like to term an "after-college dropout."

I holed myself up in my place, depleted my savings, and fell into a horrible depression whose genesis I didn't fully understand. Then, my brother Doug, who had never really found a direction in life saw an ad for work in the Grand Canyon for the food concessionaire. So, off we went to the south rim of one of the world's seven greatest wonders. I became a minimum wage food server on a cafeteria line. This job became the first of many I worked way below my level of education from 1986-94. Yet, the depression lingered. I was unable to forgive myself for leaving that "career-starting" position. My brother and I shuttled between the Grand Canyon, Yosemite National Park, and a posh ski resort where I was a ski lift operator for two winter seasons.

Then, my step-father died at age 57 of kidney cancer on November 17, 1989. My brother had left the merry-go-round we were on and moved to Reno. After a brief, failed stint of moving back to where I was raised, I joined him in Reno where I worked for four years...first in the casinos and then for two academic years I worked on the campus of the University of Nevada-Reno as a minimum wage cashier from 1992-1994. The year 1994 began as any other, but was to become an epochal year in my life. I was sharing an apartment with my brother. Typical of a lower-income apartment in Reno we shared a kitchen with the neighbor.

My brother and I had taken in a black friend who had been fired from a casino job over Christmas 1993. The racial epithets began to fly from our Spanish neighbor. In May 1994 the food concessionaire lost the bid to renew their contract and I was laid off. I began working out of a temporary service.

Then, one Friday night we were partying in the shared kitchen with the Spanish neighbor who was an ex-boxer from the Bronx. My brother beat me up when I challenged him to stop singing two tunes. He would laugh at the repugnant racial slurs about the ex black-roommate when he thought I could not hear and then act offended when I could. I made a near-fatal miscalculation when I demanded to know in the presence of the neighbor that night as to whether our black friend was a nigger. In hindsight, I believe my brother's reaction was fueled more by fear of what the ex-boxer might do to me. Also, his response to the comments fit in with my brother's accommodating personality.

Our mother had planned a visit to us months earlier. Luck would have it that the argument had just happened; I had moved to a bush-by-the-freeway as I worked out of the temp. service to gather savings to get another place. I had told my brother not to tell our mother of my strained circumstances. He did tell her. She offered me the chance to return to Boise, live with her, and get re-established.

I hesitated to take her offer for in the intervening years since my teens we had developed 'issues' between us. Yet, I had read at the Reno library that the mother-in-law of the man who had offered me the Congressional internship I'd served years earlier as a political science major had won the Republican primary in Idaho. So, I thought: "Why not accept this offer; return to Boise; and volunteer for the campaign?" Maybe it would lead to a job offer.

Lacking construction skills or much common sense at all, I'd been working a ticket- a job that was dirty, but worked every day at the temp. service. I picked up trash at the Washoe County landfill. Our main antagonist was the plastic grocery sacks. With picker-uppers we spent 90% of our time grabbing these before the wind could blow them over to nearby Interstate 80 thus preventing drowsy drivers who had trekked hours through the Nevada desert from suddenly swerving to avoid blowing plastic grocery sacks.

As I worked this job my mind went back in time to a horrible incident fourteen years earlier. In 1980, I flew to Seattle to visit my mother's younger sister. Their older brother was living with her. She had divorced her husband and was struggling. The older brother was struggling as well, but when I flew there to visit I did not know I was flying into a hornet's nest of resentment towards my mother.

So, one day I was asking my aunt about my father. Yes, even at 19, I remained curious about my long-dead father. Yet, the questions I asked were never in the direction my aunt suddenly hurled it. She held her hand to her stomach and said: "I don't know if you had been conceived yet when your father was in Korea, but your mother had an affair with a used car salesman…"

As she said this, she held her hand to her stomach. I was stunned and scared. At that point in my life I didn't know when my father had been in Korea. For hours until I reached my mother I thought of how my brother was 6'2", Dad was 6'4"…both taller than my 6 feet tall…of how Dad and Doug were left-handed; of how all the family albums were of Doug's first walk, Doug's first poop. Yet, few photos of just me. "Oh my God, this father I loved was not my father. I was the bastard son of a used-car salesman…" I thought, "Why else would my aunt tell me such a thing?" Finally, I called my mother on vacation back in California visiting a friend.

I asked her point-blank: "Is my father my father?"

She knew immediately what I was talking about and screamed: "You were born at Fort Ord before your father went to Korea!" So, I was my father's son, but now I had to digest that a marriage and love Mom had described as special had suffered an adultery. This statement caused a rupture between Mom and her sister that lasted for years. She admitted to her affair, but without any details.

Like my father's death, this became the silent elephant in the recesses of my heart: a pain; a loss of innocence about my parents I never should have been made aware of. It also became a source of anger for me. This father's love was frozen at the age I'd lost him-five years old.

Now, as a grown man I had to entertain thoughts and images of the worst behavior a married spouse can engage in…adult questions. Also, I simmered at the idea that anyone took away even a few hours of my life-of my love for my father-with the question of whether he had fathered me at all. Emotional wounds never closed remain open and bleeding. The only way to close them is with an apology, but none was ever offered by my mother or her sister.

Thus, the stage was set. In retrospect, it almost borders on the edges of farce of how this drama played out except for the devastating consequences which resulted from it.

So, I accepted the offer to return to Boise. Within two weeks I had a job as a room service waiter. Through a friend of my mother's I was interviewing to become a stockbroker with Dean Witter and I was volunteering out of the press operation of the Chenoweth for Congress campaign.

Yes, at 33 it seemed pathetic I was living with my mother and relying on her for a ride into my job at 6 a.m. job as a room-service waiter.

Then, a tsunami of bad luck, karma, circumstance or just whatever-the-hell-it-is that rules fate in people's lives roiled through my life. The day before Labor Day weekend I lost the room-service job in one day. I could not read two room-service tickets my manager had written. I waited almost ten minutes as he jaw-boned with the business executives who were the main clientele of this upper-scale hotel and restaurant. Finally, I went on the floor to ask what his undecipherable writing meant. He exploded. Businessmen looked at their stained white shirts. His tirade had been so loud and sudden.

I immediately walked to the back of the kitchen to get this away from the customers. That afternoon I was fired. The general manager was not going to allow his restaurant manager of six years to take the fall for his own behavior.

In Idaho, one of the nation's most Republican states, the state's only newspaper had been owned for years by out-of-state national corporations. The only daily paper for Boise had, like its parent corporation, a more liberal ideological stance than its readership. I was volunteering out of the press operation for the Chenoweth for Congress campaign. This two-man paid staff was separately contracted and worked out of a separate office two blocks from campaign headquarters.

Helen Chenoweth, the challenger, was taking on the two-term Democratic incumbent-Larry LaRocco. Again, the year was 1994...the year of the Newt Gingrich led 'Contract with America'. Larry LaRocco had broken a 12 term, 24 year unbroken string of Republican control of the 1st Congressional District seat when he had ran for and won the seat vacated by Larry Craig in 1990. Larry Craig, now of Minnesota bathroom stall fame, won his first term in the Senate in 1990.

I was ideally situated. The press guys had no plans to accompany Helen to Washington D.C. if she won. Thus, who would be a natural choice for press secretary? After years in the minimum-wage wilderness a good chance existed that within six months of cherry-picking trash at the Reno, NV landfill I might be a Congressional press secretary in the nation's capitol.

Instead, the state's largest television station committed an act of political distortion and censorship that would have made Hearst proud. The Minority Whip of the U.S. Congress flew from Florida to announce special targeted funds being sent to the Chenoweth for Congress campaign. Instead, the local NBC affiliate did a close-up of the Minority Whip announcing his position on a trade bill that was high on the legislative agenda...then very brief reference was made to the real reason for his flight out from Florida to announce that Helen was one of the promising challengers in the nation most likely to take out a Democrat.

So, at the little table Mom had set out for me in the garage I wrote a memo of how Chenoweth could respond to this censorship. The next morning I made seven copies at a Kinko's print shop. Then, I went to the press office and no one was there. It was past 10 a.m. So, I walked the two blocks to the main headquarters and distributed the first five copies to the top five in the campaign hierarchy.

Finally, just past 1 p.m, the second-in-command of the press operation finally shows. I show him the memo; tell him I'd already distributed the memo to the campaign manager and the campaign's other top echelon and then I added my usual addendum: "But remember, I'm just a volunteer so circular file what you don't like."

The second wave of that year's tsunami then occurred. He blew and yelled: "Do you think you're running the press operation?"

Although I always hold steadfast for what I believe in, I don't waste my time arguing with the irrational so I turned to leave. It was only ten steps to the door of this small hole-in-the-wall office on the basement floor of this historical old 1930's seven-story office complex. As I opened the door to leave Mr. Unstable shot his last wad at me: "Get out of here! You pussy-wimp."

I walked back and said: "Guy, now you have challenged my manhood and I have to say what I want to do with your mother…"

The man who had offered me the Congressional internship twelve years earlier and was now the son-in-law of the Congressional candidate could not intervene because the press operation was separately contracted. So, like the room-service job…poof…gone was the hope I'd soon be a Congressional press secretary.

The final letdown? I had failed the last of three tests to become a Dean Witter broker. I'd missed by 6 points on a 100-point scale. Five calls to New York, I "played" the broker and offered a fictional portfolio of stocks, bonds, and mutual funds tailored to the investment objectives of the "investor" who graded my sales pitch. The problem? I got the same woman for 4 of the 5 calls. Was she a man-hating New York City feminist who sub-consciously graded me too harshly?

All of this hope and promise gone in a two-week stretch. The old 'issues' surfaced. Not able to face this sea of change in my personal fortunes, I began to argue with Mom. She said: "Take any job. You said you never want to be a graveyard sales clerk at a convenience store because you 'might' get shot in a robbery…well, if that is what you can find then that's the job you take!"

My mother was shell-shocked at the sudden turn of events. She began to think "something" must be wrong. The 1990's brought the advent of big-time victimhood. If you could not excuse your own failings or that of a family member's then find a label…a 'reason' to exonerate oneself or your loved ones.

I admitted to myself the 'old issues' were surfacing so I set up counseling for myself.

Then, the next morning I asked my mother how her sister could have cast a stone of judgment on her over her affair when two years earlier that same sister had been a high school senior- unmarried and pregnant-who had given birth to a baby that lived two weeks and died.

What happened next is under seal in records of the Ada County Courthouse. My mother threatened to call 9-1-1; to have the Boise Police Department come to her house as my penance for my impertinence. The Boise Police Department was to make TIME magazine just three years later in an article on police brutality. Frightened, I physically took my mother's hand from the phone and ordered her to sit down and calm down. That evening I came home from a temp. job to find she had left me $20 and a note: ""I've gone to stay with friends to think things over…"

It wasn't hard to figure out that she had gone to stay with the Vice-President of Dean Witter local office and his wife. Yet, when I knocked on their door they shuttered the windows and never answered the door. The next evening I got off the bus from my temp. job and from the golf hole their condo faced I yelled: "Mom, I kept the counseling session," extended my arms and said: "I love you!". They closed the blinds.

The next day I called from the bar of the private golf club after another failed visit where my ring at their doorbell remained unanswered. Fifteen minutes later a sheriff's deputy showed up at the golf course bar.

I was drinking coffee trying to figure what to do next. How could we stop this madness if she would not talk to me?

The police officer ordered me to go outside to the semi-oval entrance to the golf club. He told me to get in the back of his police car without being handcuffed. I had to have my hands free to read my mother's request for a Temporary Protection (Restraining) Order.

Once we got to her small home in an exclusive, private-gated community, the sheriff had the keys to her house. Once I stepped in he said: "Your mother set out this suitcase. You have five minutes to pack it starting now."

So, I was instantly homeless with $3.17 to my name. Why I remember that exact amount 14 years later I do not know.

I stayed at Winterhouse. This Air Force-like hangar warehoused the city's homeless, but it was in its death throes for a private foundation had built the brand-new Community House: a model three-story facility with homeless men/women on 1st floor; homeless families on the 2nd floor; and the 3rd floor could not be accessed by the 1st or 2nd floor residents. The city had saved the private foundation's dream when the foundation fell short of its fund-raising goal. The city of Boise said: "Add a third floor of Federal HUD low-income single-occupancy apartments and we will make up your funding shortfall."

This addition was to bode well for me later…but first I walked through three-and-a-half months of a shelterless, homeless winter from 11-03-94 to 2-17-95.

I refused to stay at the Christian men's Rescue Mission because an active case of TB was breathing there and I felt it was a flop-house for a lot of drunks. The moment I lost my housing I thought: "The last thing I can afford to do is cloud my mind and judgment with alcohol when I didn't know where I would sleep from one night to the next." Although an infrequent social drinker, I abstained entirely from alcohol throughout that entire homeless experience.

This brand-new Community House facility opened on November 1, 1994. As us homeless people waited for its doors to open a staffer came out to announce a local TV station planned to film only the first three people entering and they needed volunteers because of the "stigma" of homelessness.

Of all the ironies, a man bellowed back at the staffer: "I'm a Vietnam veteran. I want to go first so they can see what's happened to us!"

I piped in with: "I'm the son of a man killed in Vietnam. I want to go first so they can see what's happened to us!" I really had said it in jest, but if eyes were bullets I would not be alive today to tell this Rodney Dangerfield story of woe. The Vietnam Veteran shot me the meanest look I think I've ever seen.

Seeing the anger in his eyes I said: "Hey, guy, I'll gladly go third."

This brand new building; this Community House was later toured by HUD Secretary Henry Cisneros as a model for the new, all-inclusive treatment for homelessness. It housed homeless men and women on the 1st floor; had 40 units for homeless families on its second floor and case managers for each shelter resident…except the city had saved the completion of the project by having the architect revise the original two-story design by adding a 3rd floor accessible by a special elevator and stairwell key. Here were small Single Room Occupancy apartments where renters paid below-market rates. Failure to pay meant eviction.

On the third night I was lined up to see if I was going to pay $2.00 for my bed space or mop floors or clean toilets to "earn" my cot.

When it was my turn I said: "Gary, I have $2.00, but a concern. I know you guys are new, but the staff is talking down to us real bad... like we're children. I'm homeless, but I'm a homeless man: not a child."

His response rang in my ears for the next 100 days and nights. "You will stop your bad-mouthing and smarting off or I will kick you out of here and you will have nowhere to go! Do you understand me?" As he bellowed this reply, he stood up from his chair and waved his finger two inches from my nose.

Aghast at his response I realized this new facility was going to give me a cot to sleep on, but strip me of my self-respect and dignity. So, I left that evening and walked into 100 days shelterless homeless where the temperature reached as low as 15 degrees at night and rarely above 40 degrees in the day.

What I experienced is a scar that will never leave...the hatred; the "Get a job, asshole!" and being thrown from restaurants for no reason but my beard and dirty coat offended the visual sensibilities of the housed. Perhaps, someday I will write a book about those 100 days 'in-winter'. Just as a solider-veteran knows the day he arrives 'in-country' I know my 'in-winter' dates.

What saved me from this living Hell? The writing talent I had yet to learn my father had passed on to me.

Three times after a two-and-a-half hour walk from downtown to the only 24 hour coffee shop I nearly killed myself. I had to cross a freeway overpass at the end of this 'icicles-on-my-chin and beard' two hour trek. I'm proud I remained goal-oriented even down to when I thought of making the jump from the overpass to the freeway. I told myself that I would time the jump so I would kiss a trucker's windshield and die that way instead of splatting like a tomato on the freeway pavement.

I did not see my father's letters until another year-and-a-half had passed. What saved me and forged the devotion to write this book?

"If my father could go to Vietnam and do what he did, then I-as his son-could handle this. Bring it on you motherfuckers!" That thought saved me three times.

Since we were pulled out of church after dad's death I have struggled with questions of faith all my life. As iconic and well-known as Norman Rockwell's portrait of an American family at the dinner table is the simile of the "Footprints in the Sand" where the Lord carried one whose strength was gone. From a view above the beach a person has a conversation with God. There is a long trail of two sets of footprints imprinting the sand. Yet, the trail is broken…there is a portion where there is only one set of footprints.

So, the Lord explains: "Don't you know that when you had no strength left, I carried you."

As you will read, I had no God. Shortly after my father was killed; my brother and I were taken out of church. The loss of her mother when she was 6 to breast cancer; the sudden heart attack and death of her "Daddy" when she was 18 and then the loss of her husband at age 27 in the jungles of Vietnam overwhelmed my mother.

From 11-03-94 to 12-16-94 I survived by asking for odd jobs at businesses. Then I was arrested for that 'crime.' I sat dejected and handcuffed in the back of a Boise police cruiser, but exploded into rage when the officer waiting to transport me called me "a piece of shit."

I leaned forward and hopefully busted his left ear-drum as I screeched: "my father did not die in Vietnam so you could call me a piece of shit." I then leaned back and kicked the plastic divider between front of squad car and back like a drowning man. Officers opened the door and maced me-its pungent strength robbed me of the ability to breathe and I stopped my kicking. Once again, just as with the Protection Order hearing where I had said: "my father died in Vietnam and I share his name…to bring that name into this Court under this hysterical claim of abuse…" I had planned those comments. Just where the exhortation "my father died in Vietnam!" came from in my blind rage at being called a "piece-of-shit" I do not know.

As I thawed in jail for three days I was unaware the BOISE WEEKLY had printed on 12-15-94 this response to an article about putting the homeless to sleep.

I cried when I read A PLACE ALONE (BW 12-8). That's OK. When I was 11 my mother told me my deceased father never thought it unmanly to cry. Where is my father? He's been in San Bruno, California for 28 years-his place looks out over the beautiful Southern Peninsula of San Francisco. My father is in Golden Gate National Cemetery. He died in Vietnam doing what he loved-flying helicopters. Whether his casket was spit upon by war protestors on his return I'll never know.

I cried again after a local church fed those the mainstream radio talk show host suggested should be put to sleep. I looked into the eyes of those homeless at the feed and saw their humanity. Aren't the eyes the window to the soul?

Then I cried one last time as I looked at the wallet-size miniature of the diploma-the bachelor's degree I got (BSU 1984) on the G.I. Bill because my country sent my father to 'Nam and only his corpse returned.

If the radio host has his way and the ovens are built in MACHT SCHNELL fashion-quickly-I will be put to sleep before I can regain a home, before I can apply again the diploma my father's death allowed me to study to gain so I could contribute to my country and honor his memory.

I am 33. I am homeless.

Now that asking for odd jobs had led to jail, I was too snake-bitten to continue that. So, I became what I recoiled at: a street beggar, but I never held a cardboard sign. In my beard and jacket I asked for spare change.

Yet, I went into the BOISE WEEKLY to ask for copies of the issue where my letter to-the-editor had appeared. The editor said: "You are a good writer. Our second annual Top 10 list issue is coming out January 5. Do us a Top Ten list on any subject. If we like it we will print it along with those of the notables in the community we've asked to do a Top 10 list."

So, on the cover of the 01-05-95 BOISE WEEKLY was a list of a bunch of well-known people in Boise, their titles followed by their names…and there I was "homeless Boisean Mark Seeley. Inside was my Top 10 list.

THE TOP TEN REASONS WHY THE HOMELESS PITY YOU
10. Because you're less likely to smile at a homeless person than a co-worker.
9. Most of you think in absolutes: "All homeless are bums," while the homeless know some of you think, "There, but for the grace of God, go I."
8. You will tithe at church and moments later deny a cold, homeless person one dollar for coffee so they can get inside somewhere…out of the cold.
7. You communicate through cowardly eye contact what you don't have the courage to say to a homeless person.
6. You know a homeless person is a bum without asking. How did you become so omnipotent and all-knowing?

5. As happened to a homeless person-if you own a business you will have a homeless person arrested for asking if they can clean toilets or wash windows-any work for two dollars- instead of begging for quarters on the sidewalk.

4. Some of you believe your newer-model car makes you worth more as a human being than the owner of a '65 Rambler...and certainly worth more than a homeless bum with no car.

3. "Love thy neighbor as yourself." Since the homeless are always on the move, aren't they everyone's neighbor? So shouldn't you love them as you love yourself?

2. Pets on Parade-type shows allow people to see which dogs they might want to give a home to. Where is such a public-service show for the human strays wandering in the cold? Is it that in our society dogs deserve shelter more than the human homeless?

1. Jesus washed the feet of his disciples. Would you ever offer to wash a homeless person's clothes?

Mark Seeley is a homeless person in Boise

I don't remember the exact date the light bulb went on in my head. Disgusted at being a street beggar, I came upon an idea: "Print up copies of my Top 10 list and ask quarter donations. If someone declined they would still get the Top 10 list."

So, from about a week after the 01-05-1994 publication to 02-21-1995 this is how I survived.

Even in that living Hell, life had its moments. Before I became homeless I had sent a letter of condolence to Senator Craig's chief of staff after hearing his mother had died. When I had interned for the first term Congressman in his local office in 1982, Greg was a lower-level Washington D.C. aide.

Since the Protection Order was in force the only way I could receive my mail was through my counselor. About a week before I received his thank-you letter on Senatorial letterhead I had-in my beard and jacket-told some shelter-homeless guys playing pool at the bar that served me coffee from 9p.m.-2a.m. that I had been a Congressional intern 12 years earlier. One of them in particular got angry at what he saw as a ridiculous claim and lie from a homeless man.

A few weeks later my counselor turned over mail Mom had given her, included was the Chief-of Staff's card of thanks that began "No apologies needed for kindness. I am better with faces than names…"

So, the next time I saw that guy playing pool I whipped out the letter, pointed to the postmark and return address on the envelope and said: "See this? I did intern for Craig."

A few weeks later I was at a Boise institution having coffee. It was a restaurant downtown known as Moon's Kitchen. It was famous for how politicos from the nearby State Capital would gather in back. Who walks in? Senator Craig's chief-of-staff back from Washington D.C. I turned and said: "Greg…I got your thank-you letter."

He looked at my dilapidated appearance and said: "John (the Congresswoman-elect's son-in-law) told me what happened to you. Look, I'm meeting with some Democrats in the back. Come over to the Senator's office at 1p.m. I can make 15 minutes for you. Let's talk."

So, that afternoon we met. We talked in a conference room. At one point the Senator's main secretary knocked on the door and said: "Greg, its Washington calling…"

Greg replied: "Tell Washington I'll call back. I need ten more minutes with Mark."

Our conversation ended with his offer. "Mark, I can't help you out of this, but look us up for the 1996 re-election effort. I might have a job for you." So, I got up in my beard and jacket stained with my shelterless battle to survive and walked back into that winter at least heartened that someone of his stature cared.

Ironically, a few weeks later I was peddling my Top 10 list right outside the Borah Post Office where the first-term Senator had his offices. Greg must have been back in Idaho again on business. It was snowing that day. He walked by me with a group from the Senator's office...probably headed to lunch.

I spotted him and said: "How about this acronym for the '96 re-election effort:
"CRAIG- C-ongressional R-esponsibility A-nd I-ntegrity (in) Government...C.R.A.I.G. "

He smiled and said: "Definitely look us up in '96"

I never did. Why? The cruelest people to me that winter for that month I asked donations on my published Top 10 list were the executive-suited businessmen. Generally conservative, these men sang the praises of free enterprise and self-initiative. Here I was trying to subsist on nothing but food stamps and my own initiative asking donations on my list, but they shunned me like I was a leper.

One afternoon the editor of the BOISE WEEKLY spotted me asking for 25 cent donations for reprint copies of my "Top Ten Reasons Why the Homeless Pity You" and asked how much money I was making.

The next issue of BW had short AP like news bites on Page 3. Under an article on then-Governor Batt and the state's Department of Environmental Quality position on nuclear waste shipments was the headline: "Will Write for Food." The article said my "Top 10 Reasons Why The Homeless Pity You" list could not be found in bookstores or on-line, but could be obtained on the streets where I was asking one-quarter donations and averaging $3.00/hr. in profits.

Then, on the Friday before President's Day weekend I was downtown. I had not walked the two hours out to the Airport Denny's, I don't know why. Yet, I was trying to raise coffee money. A downtown sandwich shop opened at 6:30 a.m. So, about 6:00 a.m. I started asking for donations on my list. A police officer pulled over. I retreated and stood against the wall of a bank building. He got out of his squad car and said: "I got a report of a pan-handler downtown."

"No sir. I ask donations on this list published in the BOISE WEEKLY. If you don't give me anything; you still get the list."

He scrunched his face up. I imagine he was all cock-sure set to arrest me, but just learned I was not soliciting by virtue of my donation system. He then said: "Cease-and-desist until you go to City Hall to see if you need a vendor's license. If I see talking to anyone-I'll arrest you."

Thank God-or whatever decides one's fate because I counted my change up and discovered I had 69 cents to my name. Coffee at that shop was 65 cents plus tax!

This officer's attempt to abort my pitiful subsistence led that day to a chain of events that got me housed. I did go to City Hall, but never went to the vendor's bureau.

I detoured and walked into the Mayor's office. In my four month growth of beard and dirty street coat I sat across from the Mayor's secretary and said: "A police officer told me to come here to City Hall to see if I need a vendor's license to ask one quarter donations on this list I had published in the BOISE WEEKLY. How is it going to look if the media gets hold of the fact the city bureaucracy is requiring a homeless man to pay $25 or $50 to ask for quarter donations to survive?"

She got up without a word and left the room. I was convinced she was too frightened to pick up her phone and call the police on me right in front of me. Yet, I had done nothing wrong. I was a citizen with a grievance so I remained seated. I'd had numerous encounters with the police over these 100 days and nights.

The Mayor's secretary returned with a man in a three-piece suit. He waved me into an adjoining conference room with a long table. We sat down at the end nearest the door.

He said: "Tell me about yourself."

So, for at least fifteen minutes I told him the whole tale of woe. Then he said: "How about if the city of Boise were to offer you one month's rent for a third floor apartment at Community House. If you don't pay the second month's rent you will be evicted. This will give you a chance to get back on your feet."

I said: "Excuse me sir, but I've only been able to get food stamps. I'm not a welfare father who can attach myself to my child and get housing and food. I'm not a criminal out of prison with a halfway house to go to; I'm not substance-addicted with a treatment program to be admitted to; I'm not mentally ill (I was not diagnosed with manic-depression until later that year). I've fallen through the cracks and only heard why nothing can be done to help me. You are offering to help me?"

"Yes. I'm the director of Boise's Housing and Community Support Division, I've been following your homeless writings in the BOISE WEEKLY and I always wanted to help you. I just never knew who you were. I've read what you've written about respect and dignity and understand why you refuse to stay in the shelters."

We left almost immediately for Community House so he could explain to the third floor manager that all credit checks and normal procedures were to be ignored and a third floor apartment was to be readied for my occupancy.

However, on the way over he stopped to buy himself a pack of cigarettes and asked if he could buy me a pack. Once he returned to the car he said: "One of the reasons I wanted to help you was that letter-to-the-editor you wrote. My father came home from World War II 80% disabled, but he came home. Your dad didn't come home from a different war."

Of course that hit me square in the solar plexus. I looked up at the roof of his car and mouthed silently to myself: "Thanks, Dad."

So, yes, my father's spirit drew close to me or I drew close to his example, but not only did my father carry me where there was one set of footprints in the snow…but it can be argued he not only carried me when I had no strength, but my writing of what he had done for our country had provided me the housing that lifted me out of that animal-like desperate existence. No life was possible in that Hell-and once there-ways out are few. With housing I had hope again. I got a job and rebuilt a life.

Humpty-Dumpty rebuilt a modest life for myself…I continued to rent the below-market rate single-room occupancy apartment the Director of Boise's Housing and Community Development had secured for me. Yet, I had a thicket of legal and behavioral health issues to run the gamut of. Included was pleading guilty to the crime of calling Mom to let her know I was out of the 20-40 degree Winter 1994-'95.

One month before I obtained housing the Protection Order was up for its 3 month expiration in January 1995…still homeless I had written a bitter petition to the Court asking it be extended. Instead of three months, the judge extended it one year to January 1996.

Thus, I knew I was breaking the law when I called her. Yet, I was in contact with a co-worker of hers and knew she was losing weight and taking anti-depressants. My tone was anything but friendly, but for her physical health I wanted her to know I was out of the cold. She waited over a month and turned the call into the Court when she "thought" I was not pursuing counseling and mental health treatment she thought I needed. In fact, I was but that did not obviate the crime of calling her.

So, as I traversed this counseling and Court road I did something I felt would help me heal from the wounds of that winter. I walked along Boise's Greenbelt where walkers and joggers and bicyclists were enjoying the Spring's beauty and I asked $1.00 donations on all four BOISE WEEKLY writings.

I fell behind on my rent, but knew the top dog of city housing was behind me. Yet, by August a meeting was held. I was told I had a week deadline to get a job…then a payment plan for the accumulated back-rent would be worked into my monthly payments for my single-room occupancy apartment.

I secured a job as a prep-cook at a downtown bar & grill in September 1995. I told no one of my homeless experience for the first six months. I wanted to cement in their minds my work ethic before I told anyone I had been a member of America's lowest-class: the homeless.

Once I finally told them the whole Rodney Dangerfield's story they were floored by the fact I was the author of the "Top Ten Reasons Why the Homeless Pity You." Apparently, they posted it on an employee bulletin board that winter after its Jan. 5, 1995 publication and had fierce debates about its message of compassion. Why? Two doors over was the bar most popular with the homeless sub-set of citizens who held cardboard signs and then would take their 'earnings' at day's end and drink them away.

Finally, in January of 1996, the Protection Order expired. It's no coincidence my brother was invited to move back to Boise just days before its expiration. I was set on not talking to my Mom ever again but one evening two days after its expiration I got home from my job to find a message on the board my brother had come by and would try again within an hour of me.

For almost an hour he lobbied me vigorously to at least meet with Mom. I recounted the 100 days of Hell that ended 11 months earlier; of her prosecution of me. All of his arguments fell flat.

Then, I looked at a favorite portrait of Dad. The same portrait I would look at when I went through my 'crying about Dad' stage when I was 11-12 yr. old. I had it leaned against the wall on top of a small dresser. I looked at him peering confidently out of an H-21 helicopter and asked myself: "What would Dad think if he knew the family his death in Vietnam had not allowed him to return to could not sit down at a table and discuss their differences?"

Then in August of 1996 my brother paid an unannounced visit. I was in the smoking yard relaxing after work when he walked up with the hint of tears in his eyes and said: "Mark, we need to go somewhere and talk."

Chapter 4: "I Could Only Bear to Read a Few"

After what seemed like a long amount of time we finally reached the coffee shop. He had moved back to Boise in January 1996 and was living with Mom. Now, it was August 1996 and Mom was on vacation visiting a sister in Colorado…not the evil sister; not the sister who had shared with me the fact my mother had been unfaithful to Dad...no, this was her older sister.

On the ten-minute drive to the restaurant I was badgering my brother. "Is Mom ok? Has she been in an accident? What's going on?"

Very tersely my brother said: "Shut up! I'll tell you at the restaurant-I can't drive and talk about this."

I'm prone to anxiety and worst-case thinking. I don't know if it was the sudden loss of Dad; Mom's cancer, that sudden Hellish toss into homelessness less than two years earlier-but reflexively I steeled myself for the worst for the rest of the drive and while we waited behind two other parties to be seated.

Finally seated, I glared at my brother. I was on the verge of anger thinking whatever was upsetting him shouldn't leave me waiting all this time...thinking the worst. I said: "For God sakes what's this all about?"

His eyes looked sunken and sad. "When Mom left for Colorado two days ago she plopped down all these letters our father wrote home from Vietnam. I could only bear to read a few…but Mark he wrote a lot like you write and the things you care about are the things he cared` about."

"Wait a minute, brother-that's not fair. I could read these letters and see you in him." I was stunned by what he had told me and upset he would spook me by saying I was like Dad.

"Well, do you want to go over to her house and read them?" Doug asked.

"Doug, you know in the nine months Mom and I have been communicating I have yet to go over to that house because of the pain it represents...it's the one place I couldn't go that winter. And, does Mom want me to see these letters?" I asked.

"Mark, I don't care if she wants you to read them...you're as much his son as I am," my brother replied with a firmness and resolve in his voice I rarely heard.

I took the convenient escape route...one that would take my away from these letters...buy me some time to think this out: to hear stories about Dad was one thing, but him in his own words? This was too close, too real to just plunge into.

About two months later-Thanksgiving Day 1996-we had a traditional Thanksgiving Dinner over at Mom's house. It was the first time I'd been in her house in over two years. At the end of the evening Mom gave me the letters.

I took them home that evening. The first thing I did was count them...this would be the only time I would have with him...or so I thought. Actually, the Korea letters that open the book were found in the pine box five years later. As you will read a few other letters surfaced as well, but at the time I couldn't know that. I opened the first letter noticing its date: March 25, 1966. He was killed on June 27, 1966...some quick math told me 55 letters in about 90 days.

My niche in the family had always been I was the family writer. Though I had not pursued it as a career there had been the SEELEY TRIBUNE, TRI-CITY SCOOP, and the homeless writings that had lifted me into a single-room occupancy apartment.

When I was a kid, I'd been shown my father's drawings and sketches. One of Grandad's stories that kept Doug and I tethered to the memory of our KIA father was how Grandad took his then-12 year old boy and his drawings to the Pasadena Art Institute. His work was passed along to art students in a class that was set to sketch a live nude sitting on a stool. Despite his sensitive age, the class voted his talent was enough for him to sit in and sketch this completely nude woman.

When I was a teenager Mom was sitting in the bean bag chair as I walked by her to the kitchen. With a far-away look in her eye she said to my brother. "Oh, your father used to write me the most beautiful letters from Vietnam."

I remember sniffing at that comment as I passed by and thinking: "Yeah, what war widow doesn't believe her husband's letters were beautiful?"

He was a gifted writer. Beyond the talent here was the heart and character of my father. Contrary to my image of him as a hard-edged Army soldier-pilot, he revealed himself as a tender, caring man.

Very early on in reading the letters, I knew they were not going to remain private. For in one of his letters came my chance to do what his death in Vietnam had denied me: work on a father-son project "with him."

In the letter he wrote: *"Honey, they have a monthly and an annual...it's called Writer's Digest/Guide. Its the Annual I want. Could you find me a copy and airmail it over to my tent. See what you can do for me. Will ya? Thanks."*

I read that passage and said out loud to no one but me and the four walls: "All right Dad-let's do it!"

The BOISE WEEKLY had asked me to write for them on other subjects after my homeless writings got me housing. I had told them: "No thanks, I only write about what I care about."

This I cared about. In December of 1996 I went to the editor of the BOISE WEEKLY. The editor from the homeless writings last published in April 1996 was gone. The new editor did not know me. So, I took my homeless writings and a few of Dad's letters and told him I wanted to let my father tell his story in his own words from excerpts of his letters, but I had one non-negotiable demand: the by-line had to be "by John S. Seeley as told by his son Mark."

The editor-David Madison-said: "Conditionally I'll agree to that as long as I don't feel your misleading the reader. Let's do this piece for our Memorial Day week issue 1997."

From December 1996 to the end of March 1997 I read and re-read his letters. After reading them all in chronological order, I would take them out randomly and read them. Somehow, it made them new again...like randomly picking gifts hanging on a Christmas tree.

Around the beginning of April 1997, I began our father-son project in earnest. I started by taking 5 letters a day to work and then going to the neighboring bar after work, drinking coffee, and making notes of his letters. Blessed with 55 letters, this process took two full work weeks. It was a joy.

As you will see my father's journey in Vietnam took him many places. So, I had to choose his most profound writings that also fit the chronology of his journey to Panel 8E Line 101 of the Vietnam Veterans Memorial.

The BOISE WEEKLY is a free advertiser supported paper. I met with the editor in early April. He gave me a maximum word count of 2,000 words for the piece.

I finished the rough draft in late April and arranged a family meeting over at Mom's house in the private-gated neighborhood she lived in. I wanted my mother and brother to read the rough draft. Anything they did not want would be edited out. Also, I wanted us to choose a title for the article from his words. The BOISE WEEKLY planned to run it as their feature piece so a photographer would need to come out to the house to take a picture. For the picture, the only place for material was the beautiful pine box Grandfather had built that held the flag that had draped his coffin 31 years earlier; his medals; and other things Grandad had lovingly preserved in this box. Grandad had died in the mid-80's. His first wife, my father's mother had died of a sudden heart attack in 1956. His second wife was always Grandma to me. She died of old age and Grandad lost his will to life and died within months of her. Upon his death in 1985 Mom drove to California, picked up the pine box, and brought it to the home she shared with my step-dad.

So, it had not been opened since Grandad's passing in the mid-80's its contents held too much pain for Mom, Doug, and I. Yet, now there was a good reason to open it: my father was to be the feature writer of a Memorial Day piece.

Before we opened the pine box I had my mother and brother read the article. I opened the article…connected the dots…and let my father's writing shine.

Doug read it first and saw nothing he had any problem with. Mom read it and made one fateful comment about what I had written about what little I knew about the crash, but other than that had no problems either.

My brother withdrew to the kitchen as I asked about a title. Neither had any immediate suggestions for the title. Mom then said: "Well, Mark you have been working on this. What do you think?"

I answered: "What Dad wrote that surrounds where he conveyed to you the words "Hell, I'm No Hero…" define the character of the man. But what he wrote to you in his first letter from Vietnam in the words that surround 'Angel, I Write These Things' define his heart."

Mom thought for just a moment and said: "Yeah, I like that because the letters were to me."

When we first opened the box, Dad's flag was on top. Yet, what caught my eye made my heart soar. On the roof of the box was a beautiful painting of a flight of Chinooks-a wave of five with one dislodging troops and four others flying in to let troops out the back on a combat assault. Not only had I been looking for some photo of a Chinook 47 to give the reader a visual reference of what the helicopter Dad flew in Vietnam looked like, but also this could be Grandad's contribution to his son's article. I'd been frustrated by the knowledge I could have done this project years and years earlier when Grandad was alive…if only I'd known about the letters.

So, we picked out his dog-tags, his Captain's bars and beret, but then came upon a colored version of a photo I'd seen many times, but only in black-white...our last family portrait at Fort Benning. I locked on to Dad's eyes and felt a physical sensation I have never had before or since. I saw the tenderness and love in his eyes and a feeling like warm water starting at the top of my head and exiting my toes washed over me. Somewhere, deep in the recesses of my memory, I'd seen these eyes before in color...in life.

Other things were found that raised troubling questions that were to transform my own priorities and direction in my life, but they concern my father's death.

Its best to first celebrate the legacy my father left by reprinting Angel, I Write These Things..." by John S Seeley as told by his son Mark.

64

Angel – I Write These Things May 22-28, 1997 issue

By John S. Seeley as told by his son Mark

©Mark Seeley

The letters that comprise this article have a simple but powerful truth to tell. It's not the image that Hollywood has portrayed and profited from, but rather the words of one good man, one officer who flew helicopters in Vietnam, a 34-year-old my captain whose 12 years of service to his county' now required him to serve in a remote base camp in Vietnam called Phu Loi, near the border to Cambodia. These letters are generously shared here by my mother who, at that time, was his 27-year-old wife.

He sailed away to Vietnam in late February of 1966. Circumstances will never permit me to forget his departure. After a brief tour of the aircraft carrier he was to sail over on we returned to the family car. He reached through the open window, enveloped my 5-year-old body in his 6'4" frame hugging me so hard I could barely breathe, did the same with my 7-year-old brother Doug, exchanged some tender words and kisses with my mother and then walked away. His first letter from Phu Loi in Vietnam left no doubt his base ramp was in the thick of things:

March 25,1966

Phu Lui, Vietnam

My Darling,

Charlie had a surprise planned for us. He tried-hard. We were routed out of bed at 11 p.m. to standby to evac aircraft to Bien Hoa. None of us could sleep from the artillery noise anyway, so got up and milled around for a while before it was decided that things were O.K What had happened was a bunch of Viet Cong in R.V.N. clothing had walked into an R.V.N. compound south of here and had captured 17 half-tracks and were thinking about coming up here for a jangle. Artillery cleared them out long before they got up here. About 42 of them. You might have heard about it on TV or elsewhere back there. We don't get any news at all over here.

Angel - I write these things in the light that I think of them - as they happen and without any relish or other garbage. But not to worry you. I have no taste for any of this at all and wish I were a lifetime away from here, aware of nothing but my wife and children around me and let the world blow itself crazy, but I'm not and I have 11 months of it yet-as of tomorrow, and so I'll watch it as it happens and tell you some of it once in awhile...

This first letter from Nam shows he received an immediate introduction to the reality that this was a different kind of war, where the enemy was often the people he was sent over to defend. Idealistic notions die fast under such conditions and his focus became singular - to do his duty and return home. That duty, as a pilot of the Army's main transport helicopter, the twinrotor Chinook 47, began just after his arrival in Phu Loi as a letter written just a week later attests:

April 3, 1966

Phu Loi, Vietnam

My Darling

Today, I flew on one of our first operational missions. Nothing hard really, but after we had been gone only 5 hours I was whipped. It is a struggle simply to fly in the heat and dust. The carrying of personnel, armor, survival gear, canteen, helmet, maps. and etc. into the cockpit is, in itself a staggering task. To climb into the cockpit, over and around the "Iron Maiden" exhausts one completely.

The "Iron Maiden", is an armor sheath that locks over the body after entrance into the seat. Opened, it makes cockpit entrance almost impossible. Once closed, it makes availability of circuit breakers (and we have hundreds, above, below, on back on all sides) switches, levers and so on times impossible. It would preclude the fast - or even slow exit from the aircraft in the event of a crash. Yet, it is designed to protect the vital body organs from at least a .30 caliber round. I will wear it closed on a combat assault for sure, but the rest of the time, to hell with it. I fly with it open.

Today was a typical ash & trash haul up to Lai Khe - only a short flight from here. We hauled Connex containers and our total haul today was 32,070 LBs, 13 passengers, 12 sorties and one internal load of lumber that damned near ruined the whole aircraft. At the end of the day we had 4 major write-ups in the log book for and even though we get shot at on the maintenance people, had almost crushed our crew chief and were groggy form the radio noise.

Radio! My God! There are so many radio transmissions going on all the time that my mind was reeling from them. Everywhere we fly we have to dodge our own artillery and the job of finding a landing zone becomes a major life-or-death matter trying to sneak through our own fire - especially with radios that quit working at the most crucial moment. –

Since we have only now become operational, many things have to be ironed out -for months to come, before we can get things down pat. By the time we had shut down for the last time today I had learned a lifetime of experience and was drenched with sweat and dust until it hurt to close my eyes -for the dirt in them.

Yet, it remains a war of contrasts.

I went to the mess tent and picked out two steaks to grill myself (a regular Sunday night affair) and had a dinner that would have cost $12.00 back in the States. I was too tired to eat it later and came here to the tent to watch the floor for an hour and smoke cigarettes…. You wrote and asked if there was a safe place at all in Vietnam. No darling, there isn't anywhere at all. I'm safer here than I am with 4 people in a jeep in Saigon. The men down in the motor pool are on the crucial edge of our perimeter and even though we get shot at on final approach into the airstrip, I would rather have that than sleep down by the trucks at night. Sweetheart, I'm too tired to write another line. I'll sleep this night.

Infinity,

John

Though his mind and body were fully engaged in the war around him, his heart remained at home. Replying to one of the many letters mom wrote to him he said in an April 27, 1966 letter:

Of all your descriptive narratives I have read thus far, none has touched me so deeply nor made me long for the sight and 'touch of all of you - as much as did your description of our son Doug walking to and home from school. Yes, I believe that he sang most of the way and stopped to sit down to look at his books – my precious first-born son. How I long to hold him in my arms and watch his innocent eyes as he seeks the answers to all his curiosity about his world around him. These moments that we can spy on their world make us fortunate thieves, as innocent as them, and we are cleansed of any of the worldly knowledge that makes us adult and sadder for it. Steal every moment you can of these golden years my love, for there is nothing so dear in our roles as parents as these rewards...:

Not only was he dealing with the adjustment to Nam, but he felt bedeviled by the kidney stones which led him on an odyssey out of Vietnam to a base hospital in Japan. He had a one-day layover at Clark Air Force Base in the Philippines where he wrote of a delay in leaving the Saigon airport. From his descriptions, it's obvious his condition was much less serious than many of the patients.

May 20, 1966

Clark Air Force Base,

Philippines

...The convoy of ambulances got out to Tan Son Nhut airport at 4:00 pm. and the aircraft for our evac came in and had to take an hour to refuel - at this time it was discovered by attending hosp ital personnel that the plane was not going to depart for the Philippines because of a typhoon so they had to pull all the patients into a staging area over night rather than return them to the hospital in Saigon. It was crowded but better than I expected - much like a front-line battalion aid station.

The wounded — the seriously wounded were placed in beds and attended to first and I did what I could to help the corpsmen make them comfortable as possible. At first we were told we would evac early the next morning. I helped as many as I could, feeding them or cutting meat for them. Since I was in uniform and was wearing my rank, many would wonder just what the hell a Captain-pilot was doing walking around the ward and I would have to explain I was a patient too.

I don't know how to say this to you darling - but I felt guilty for even being there with a full and whole body - and I still feel this way. I am being honest with you - I am in a God-damned war and I intend to survive, but the sights I have seen as a pilot - of wounded - and then last night in that shelter - men torn to shreds with tubes running into them - casts seeping blood - the faces and eyes of these kids, has infuriated and humbled me. These people knew that they were going home to the States and were not unhappy about it. Yet, I saw some cry because they were worried about the squad they were leaving behind and they would call out names to see f their buddies - wounded at the same time - in the same action were there with them.

The Chief Doctor came around to me finally and asked how I felt. I was weak, but more than that I needed a drink and wanted to go over to the Air Force Officers Club. He told me I had earned it and rounded up two officers to accompany me over there. The place was mobbed with pilots - some who fly a lot, some who seldom get off the ground. I sat at a table and could tell what stories were real and who had a right to be drinking. I didn't get drunk. I had about 6 scotch & sodas over a 4 hour period I sat with one Air Force pilot who was ready to turn in his wings because - thru no fault of his own - he had dropped ordnance on our own troops. I didn't tell him that some of the men in my ward were those he had hit, but just let him talk it out. Then someone remembered it was Ho Chi Minh's birthday and we all stood and sang:

"Happy Birthday to You, Happy Birthday to You, Happy Birthday, Ho Chi Minh, Happy Birthday - FUCK YOU!"

The end of the song heralded the smashing of glasses and bottles against the wail and the club manager declared free drinks for all. Quite a blast. I had one more drink and found my way back to the shelter where I stayed up all night talking and lighting cigarettes for the serious cases. By the time the sun had come up - I didn't feel tired at all – and for the first time in days felt as though I was a man again - on my feet.

We got off on time this morning and I slept most of the way over here. They weren't sure we could even make it in here (to the Philippines) because of the typhoon, but here we are and tomorrow - if the typhoon permits we will be evaced to our different destinations. Mine will be Camp Drake in Japan...

The tangled web of mistakes which led to this trip were explained in a letter he wrote from Camp Drake just before returning to Vietnam. When he was initially treated for kidney stones in a field hospital in Bien Hoa, Vietnam, he contracted bronchitis. Doctors put him on contradictory medications which wreaked havoc with his system. However, a physician in Saigon took him off all these medications, but he had already been processed out to Japan.

Thus, once at Camp Drake, he was no longer taking the medications that caused the problems and the medical doctors there could find nothing physically wrong. So, as a final precaution, they sent him to see the base psychiatrist. The doctor found him normal, which is all Captain Seeley would accept anyway. Dad wrote of the doctor's findings:

. . he feels I'm an interesting case for a normal Individual since he is especially interested in pilots. I'm the first one to come through his office that was trying to get back to Vietnam, all the others were trying to get out of going back. Hell - I'm no hero and damned sure don't want to go back and get shot at - who does? I made sure he understood that. It's just that I'm there and will have to stay there until I can come home. I have accepted that and there are no shades of gray there. Anyway -for all of this trip – I got a free "bug doctor" consultation and some decent chow...

He returned to Vietnam shortly after this June 3, 1966 letter. He was killed on June 27,1966. Just as his letters betray Hollywood's version of Vietnam that rarely was, so did his death. No climactic John Wayne moment of being shot down by enemy fire undid his life. No, he was co-piloting a CH-47 on a mission to transport captured North Vietnamese Army supplies. The pilot made the final decision to fly though the weight of the cargo roughly equated the maximum payload the CH-47 was designed to handle.

The ship lifted, could not gain altitude, and crashed. Seven soldiers in the cargo area escaped, and the pilot exited through a vertical Plexiglas window to his I in the cockpit. My father, immobilized by some injury to his legs, could not get out,. By the time the others realized he had not made it out safely, it was too late. The craft was in flames.

Was my father a hero? No, not really. Certainly no more heroic than the other 58,208 who made the ultimate sacrifice in Vietnam. Yet, there is something heroic in these letters home. He had a gift for expressing the commonplace: a man's love for his family, concern for his fellow soldiers and through his struggles and choices in the last months of his life, a testimony to the meaning of the words duty.., honor.., country. There's a quote by the late Supreme Court justice Oliver Wendell Holmes I've taped above a cherished photo of my father at home. Perhaps this says it best:

"At the grave of a hero we end,

Not with sorrow at the inevitable loss,

But with the contagion of his courage,

And with a kind of desperate joy - WE GO BACK TO THE FIGHT."

Indeed, Dad, indeed.

Captain Seeley's widow and two sons all live and work in Boise. Mark Seeley is a contributing writer to Boise Weekly.

Editor's Note: Questions have arisen surrounding the crash that killed Captain Seeley. A Congressional inquiry was requested by the family and is currently being conducted through the Pentagon.

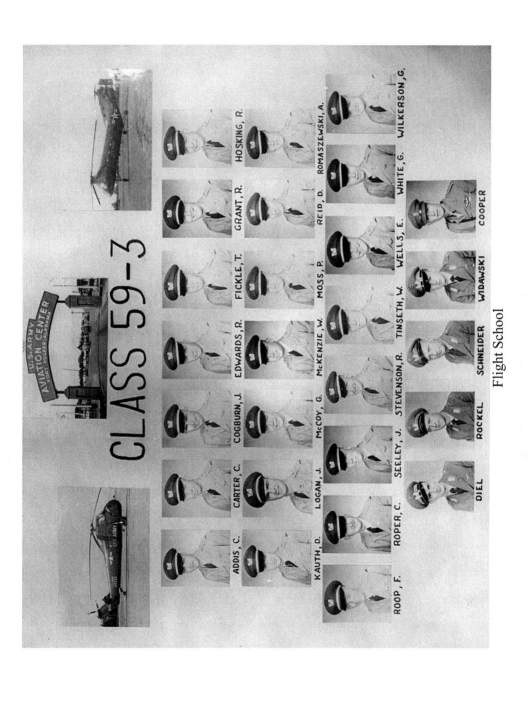

Flight School

Doug, Mark, Alice, and John
Last family portrait Ft. Benning, Georgia 1965

Military Policeman 1953

Piloting H-21 Helicopter near Fort Ord, CA, 1959
Army aviator John S. Seeley logged 1,297 hours in his 1959-66
abridged career. 1,205 hours were logged in the H-21.

Co-Piloting an H-21Korea 1961

Korea 1961

Robert Remsberg and John Seeley, on the balcony of the Pacific Hotel,
VUNG TAU, RVN March 1966.

178th "Boxcars" Flight Line at Phu Loi, RVN

Wreckage of Boxcar 162

Memorial Service at Phu Loi, RVN

Memorial Plaque
Nevada City, CA

Taps

Medals Ceremony Mather AFB February 1967

178th "Box Cars" Unit Patch
Medals

Chapter 5:"...But I Don't Know About How Quickly"

For thirty years I'd wondered about this giant of a man who had imprinted on me a love I did not understand, but after reading his letters gone was my guilt of not being able to 'let go'. The ferocity of that final hug good-bye finally made sense. Ever since his death, I'd known the love I felt in that final moment. Yet I could not share the vividness and detail of that moment fully with the readers of "Angel, I Write These Things…" for I did not tell them of his death until the end of the article.

Thus, I withheld from them all I remember of that goodbye. I didn't want the reader to pause to ask themselves: "Wait a minute. He remembers the smell of his father's uniform as his little nose was in the crook of his father's neck; he remembers tears creasing his father's cheek as he looked out the car window after regaining his breath; he remembers how overcast the sky was behind his father that day. Why would a 5 year old remember all of this?" I wanted the reader to read of the passion for life John Seeley had alive and not stop reading the article or read the article thinking all along: "this is a dead man's letters." It's why you read: "these letters were generously shared by my mother, who at that time, was his 27 year-old wife." Of course, I hoped the reader would interpret that to mean they had divorced later in life.

Now, through these letters he had come alive somehow. No, I couldn't reach out and touch him, but in holding in my hands these letters I had something physical that was not a photo of my dead father in some silent repose, but his thoughts as alive as he was when he wrote them.

I look back now on those months between being given the letters on Thanksgiving 1996 and that family meeting to review the rough draft of "Angel, I Write These Things" as an innocent time where he was lifted out of his grave and into my heart as a fully dimensional real human being.

Reading his letters revealed a very special father, but for the first time I tried to grasp just how Mom had gotten through such a loss. I recall asking her over the phone: "Mom, how many letters did you get after you knew he was dead?"

She replied: "I don't know Mark, but they just seemed to keep coming and coming." Then she added: "And my letters to him"…her voice broke here…" the ones he never had a chance to read came back marked "deceased" and those I did destroy. I didn't even open them…I didn't want to see the words I had written him that he never had the chance to read."

Where my mother found the strength to carry on I cannot say. It seemed so unjust to me they had fought and saved their marriage after my mother had been unfaithful to my father while he was in Korea in 1961. Her affair was clearly confirmed by a letter Dad wrote to her on May 10, 1966.

Though a scar remained my father's prose in his letters from Vietnam were just as tender and overwhelming as his anniversary letter from Korea in the opening of this book.

There is never a way to define anyone else's loss of a loved one, but my mother told me one story of just how profound a struggle she underwent. She told me it got so bad in the months following his death she decided she was going to kill herself, but that us 'boys' were her salvation. She did not want to leave us alone without any parents. Then, one night, her sorrow overwhelmed her and she decided in the morning she would take us with her by turning on the car and gassing all of us. My heart plunged as she told me this, but then she said: "The next morning I had to smile and almost laugh at myself though..."

"How could that be?" I asked incredulously.

She answered: "Because I went to the sink and looked out the window at our carport. I was so lost in my pain that night I'd forgotten I'd moved us to that apartment. I couldn't have gassed us in a garage we no longer had."

Yet, the father-son project of publishing him for a Memorial Day piece required me to close his article with how he had died for our country.

In the rough draft of "Angel, I Write These Things..." written the craft was "quickly consumed in flames."

All I had ever been told about the crash was the "surviving pilot got out through a hole in the cockpit plexi-glass window."

On that night in April 1997 my mother looked up from the rough draft of "Angel, I Write These Things..." and said: "Mark, it was consumed in flames, but I don't know about how quickly."

She recounted in detail for the first time a meeting she'd had told me as a teenager...a meeting with the surviving pilot when he returned from Vietnam through San Francisco. Mom met with him in March of 1966 halfway between our apartment north of Sacramento and San Francisco. Mom had driven down to the meeting point at a restaurant/bar along the freeway with a friend for moral support. Nervous, she belted down too many drinks waiting for the surviving pilot to arrive. He was about an hour late.

She explained how she had waved the surviving pilot off from further details once the recounting of Dad's death reached the rescue attempt and the words that the other pilot only had his bare hands and could not break open the hole he had gotten himself through to get back in and free my Dad. Dad had been the only one to die and now my mother's suspicions were being confirmed and she could not bear to hear what she had sheltered my brother and I from for over thirty years.

Wait! A rescue attempt? Dad had survived the initial impact from the crash? Years earlier at a Memorial Day function a Vietnam veteran asked in a voice laced with hostility: "Why are you here...this Memorial is for those who were killed or served in Vietnam. You don't look old enough to have been there?" He leaned forward in a challenging, aggressive fashion.

I defended myself with, "No, sir, I was never there, but my Dad died over there." His demeanor changed 180 degrees and I told him what little I knew of the crash.

He said: "The surviving pilot didn't crawl out over the cockpit and through the cockpit window. All models of Chinook have a plexi-glass window to the left of the pilot and right of the co-pilot. Your father must have been in a world of pain to not lift up his leg and kick at that window and fall out of that burning chopper."

When he said the word "world of pain" it knifed through me momentarily, but then I thought: "No, this is good...it means Dad was either dead or in shock and died quickly."

Within two weeks of the meeting over the rough draft "Angel, I Write These Things..." I initiated a Congressional Inquiry into Dad's death. It was only natural to take the inquiry through Senator Craig's office. Knowing Desert Storm veterans were struggling to get the Defense Dept. and VA to recognize maladies possible from that conflict just 7 years earlier, I arranged for two local TV stations to do Memorial Day stories on my father.

One approached him from who was John Seeley as a soldier, husband, and father. The other opened with: "Why are two Boise brothers having a Congressional inquiry conducted into their father's death in Vietnam?"

With only my mother's muddled memories hope remained there was an explanation for these troubling questions. Yet, my brother and I were interviewed for the piece and I said: "what contingency did the Army have to get back in and get a wounded man out?"

I tried to focus on the good…on the article "Angel, I Write These Things…" being published in 30,000 copies of the BOISE WEEKLY. Dad was now a published writer!

Ironically, my own homeless writings had been read by a woman responsible for Federal HUD grants to homeless programs and the day the printing press published "Angel, I Write These Things…" I served on a board with two University Professors that graded these grants and dispersed $750,000 to homeless programs throughout the State of Idaho.

So that first letter-to-the-editor and its closing came true on the same day for I had written almost two years before I read my father's letters "If the radio host has his way and the ovens are built in MACHT SCHNELL fashion-quickly- I will be put to sleep before I can regain a home, before I can apply again the diploma my father's death allowed me to study to gain so I could contribute to my country and honor his memory."

From my own writing I served on a board that contributed to my nation's efforts to help the homeless and while these University professors and I judged the veracity of these grant requests the BOISE WEEKLY was printing copies of an article that fulfilled the ambition Dad must have had when he asked Mom to airmail a writer's guide to his tent in Vietnam. I remember smiling to myself and imagining some judgmental jerk reading that letter-to-the-editor in 1994 and laughing to himself: 'Yeah, right. This homeless piece-of-shit is going to contribute to his country and honor his father's memory.'

In that homeless winter I had known only that my father had gone to Vietnam and died for our country. I did not know he had fought to get back to Vietnam when his medical maladies provided a road home to us...I did not know the sheer depth of his love for us beyond that hug goodbye.

I clung to that buoyant emotion in the weeks following the publication of "Angel, I Write These Things..," In a moment my grandfather would not have survived, for his heart would have burst with pride, I ran into our then Governor Batt downtown a few weeks after "Angel...." was published. I'd left a copy with his secretary and wrote in the margins the day "Angel, I Write These Things…" came out on the newsstands: "Dear Governor: For your service to country and dedication to the betterment of the citizens of Idaho, I'd like to share my father's story with you."

I was actually drinking coffee at a downtown bar. A band was playing jazz. Not much of a music fan, I finally turned around to discover the Governor playing what I remember to be the clarinet. When they went on break, I walked up and said: "Governor, I left a copy of my

Dad's article with your secretary. Dad was a helicopter pilot killed in Vietnam…the article told his story through his letters and…"

The Governor stopped my nervous rambling by offering a hand shake with the words: "Thanks for a beautiful story."

Then, in early July 1997, all this good feeling was torn from me. It was another chance encounter in downtown Boise that started my nose-dive into a despair and hurt whose complete remedy may forever elude me.

The reporter who had done a wonderful job on why my brother and I had initiated a Congressional inquiry yelled to me from a distance: "Mark, there is a Vietnam pilot who contacted me. He has a letter from the other pilot."

He gave me the man's name and phone number…it ends up he was a webmaster for an Internet group called the HELI-VETS; he had been a Huey pilot in Vietnam and saw the TV story on the Congressional Inquiry. He had searched for and found the surviving pilot.

We met at-where else? A deli I had turned into my after-work coffee shop.

I read the following letter sobbing uncontrollably and squared the pilot in the eye and told him I was not going to apologize for my tears...it was a horror. I felt as though this letter had reached in, torn my heart out and left the surviving arteries splaying around like broken piano wires.

27 June 1997

Dear Paul:

I received your letter and thought the 31st anniversary of the crash would be a good time to write a reply.

John Seeley was a good friend of mine as we went to Flight School together in 1958. He ended up in the half of the class (9 men) in the H-21 flight and I ended up in the H-34 flight. When we graduated in '59 I went to Ft. Knox KY and I'm not sure where John went. I met his wife at Rucker and later in 1965 at Fort Benning Ga. We formed a Chinook company and John as a Captain was the Motor Officer and I as a CWO was his assistant. We went by boat to Vietnam in February 1966 and ended up in Phu Loi about 18 miles north of Saigon.

I got a round in the hydraulic system in May 66 and went down on an operation west of Cu Chi (4 or 5 miles at a place called Trang Bang very appropriate name) While there the bad guys tried to take the Chinook from us and the 116th with Jim " Jake" Jacobs and his gun team shot up a million dollars of ammo into the area. After about 5 hours a "Dust Off" Huey came into pick up my crew chief who had been shot through the palm of his hand when we got hit. I was sitting in a ditch near the rice paddy berm and the bad guys shot up the place with 60MM mortar and nailed me in the back- I had the dubious distinction to be the 2nd man and 1st pilot wounded in the company. In the meantime John had gone to a hospital in Japan with kidney stones. I didn't fly because of the hole in my back for a few weeks and John did not fly because of the kidney stones. We both returned to flight status in June and had the lowest hours in the company so they put us together to fly every day till we caught up to the other pilots. I told all of this to you to explain what led up to John and I being together that day.

On 27 June, John and I went sent on a mission to take a bladder of contaminated fuel to a small confined area about 5 miles west of Dau Tieng which is Northeast of Tay Ninh. I made the first approach into the area and it was big enough but loaded with tree trunks the Engineers had blown down to make the LZ.

There was only one spot big enough for the Chinook. We landed and were told by the ground commander that they had captured a supply cache of rice, bikes, guns, etc. One of the items was tin sheets that we estimated, John & I, to weigh between 4 to 7 pounds. We told the crew chief to load about 1000 sheets to take out. They were to go to Dau Tieng for the villagers (probably mostly VC). The fuel was used to try and burn the rice. The bad guys were fighting to keep us from getting their supply dump with small arms and rifle grenades. We made a second trip in and out and unfortunately John broke the rear view mirror on the front bottom of the ship on an ant hill about 4 foot high. We joked about bad luck for 7 years. After the second trip out we went to Lai Khe to refuel. John called our operations to ask to cancel the mission. We felt it wasn't worth the risk to try to bring out junk. Ops told him if he thought it was too much for our skills he would send another ship. We wouldn't do that so we continued the mission. I made the 3rd trip in and we got a load of tin sheets and some bikes.

We went down in the jungle to see how much more junk they had and left in a hurry because there was a lot of shooting going on. I took the 3rd load out. The Chinook loads were limited to 8000 pounds. We didn't expect any problems on power. The trees were about 70 to 80 feet high. I had just gotten off above the 1st trees when all of a sudden the RPM started to drop off. I don't know if we took a hit in an engine or what but I had no choice but to zero the airspeed and pull full pitch when we entered the trees. I alerted the crew to hang on and we had a wild ride down. We ended up on our right side and I couldn't see because my helmet came down over my eyes. We had "Iron Maiden" seats for small arms protection and evidently the weight of John and the seat was too much for the crash. His seat came loose and he fell down over me and my left arm pinned in. I felt we were both dead men. Something told me to try and get out and I released the catch on my Iron Maiden but was still pinned in. I then released my seat belt and shoulder harness with my free right hand. Somehow I raised the load on my left up enough to pull it out.

I went out over the foot pedals and through a hole in the plexiglass nose. I don't know if I kicked a hole out or it broke during our trip through the trees. By this time the aircraft was burning pretty good. I saw that John and his seat were backwards to me with his head in the sound proofing above my seat and his legs over the throttle and radio center console. I yelled back through the hole, "Get out John, the ship is on fire." He replied, "I can't, my legs are caught..." I said, "This hole is too small and I can't get up in there to get you out." He said, "Try the top," his last words to me. The ship was really blazing by this time and ammo was cooking off in the cargo compartment. I climbed up on the honing antennae and tried to get in the left side window that was gone. The electronic compartment is on the left behind the copilot's seat and there was 10 kinds of smoke and flame coming out through the hatch. I couldn't get in there and dropped off onto the ground which was burning a little and was trying to pull the plexiglass nose out bigger but only got a few pieces broken off when I noticed that the sound proofing above John's head was on fire, I reached in enough to get the fire extinguisher off the edge of the floor and put out the fire around John's head. I then pounded the extinguisher flat trying to break out the plexiglass window. We had crashed in the perimeter between the good guys and the bad guys. Two G.I.'s came up and grabbed me and said, "Come on, it is going to blow." I asked them to help me and to give me something to break the window. One gave me his helmet and I mashed it almost flat to no avail.

About that time one of the fuel cells exploded with a roar and they let go of me and ran back into the jungle. I continued to pound with the helmet for a few more minutes when they came back and grabbed me and dragged me into the jungle. A little later a gunship dropped his guns and came in and picked me up and took me to a field hospital at Long Bien.

They x-rayed my arm and leg and released me after they found no broken bones. A Chinook came in and took me back to Phu Loi. I lost some hair and my ears were burned. I couldn't wear a helmet so got an R and R to Formosa. I continued to fly with the 178th for a few months, then got a transfer to the 147th at Vung Tau. I returned to the States in February 67 for 20 year retirement. I called Mrs. Seeley on the phone as she had written to ask to call. I rented a car and went to Sacramento to meet her and her girlfriend at a restaurant on the highway below Sacramento. I told her everything I told you. I don't know if she ever told the kids or not. I don't know if she is still alive or not. Did they move to Idaho?

Sorry, that this is so long but it seems I could not stop writing. You can tell the boys this story and give them my address and phone number.

By the way, I flew at Rucker for 5 years, '67 to '72, after I retired. One of the crew came into the ready room to see me. He was still in the service but had no ears. They had been burned off. He said he heard that I received a Purple Heart and he did not because the investigating officer declared it was an accident, not combat. I had told him the whole story. I said that all of a sudden the RPM started to go and that both torque needles were spinning so I don't know which engine had the problem. His name was CWO Keebler and he had been my upper classman. We had some bad feelings in flight school as I thought he was a pompous ass. I didn't push it but I wish I had. The crew member deserved a Purple Heart. I guess it is too late to change that. At the time I just wanted to get it over with and try to get my grief for John's loss under control. The wreckage, what was left of it was brought back to Phu Loi several days or a week later. They had to run a bunch of VC off to get it. It did have many bullet holes in it but Keebler thought the VC did that later. I don't know.

I attended the 30th reunion of the 178th at Fort Benning in 1995. I intend to go to the next one in Wash D.C. on 18 to 21 July 1997. I did not see any of the crew at the 30th Anniversary at Fort Benning. Maybe this time in D.C.

I'm retired now in Cape Cod. I used this VFW paper because it was the nicest I had. I want to use it up and I guess I will if I write long winded letters like this. If you get down this way, drop in for a visit. I have one son and he is married now and in his own home so I have two extra bedrooms.

I don't belong to the local Chapter of the Vietnam vets. I don't have long hair or an earring. They should belong to the VFW. I had joined the VHPA but dropped out to protest when they raised the dues. I may join again.

Okay Paul, I've bent your ear long enough. I'll re-read this and think about mailing it. Right now I'm going down to my VFW Post and have a beer for John.

Drop me a line if you hear where Mrs. Seeley is now.

Sincerely,

John R. Logan

Burned-to-death alive!

From a simple desire to publish my father to this? I'd just come through an unthinkable horror of my own...that homeless winter; the heartbreak of hysterical claims I'd been abusive to my mother.

Mom had warned me when I initiated the Congressional inquiry that I had better be prepared for whatever I found. Through this letter from the surviving pilot I had just had my own "meeting" with the surviving pilot just as she had over 30 years earlier.

Gone was any hope my father had died quickly and mercifully. Even if smoke had overcome him, he had suffered knowing for some minutes his death was going to be painful...knowing he would never see us again.

His sprit...his "footprints in the snow" had carried me through that homeless winter. One slip on the ice on those lonely 2 a.m. treks to that 24 hour coffee shop and I could have been found somewhere the next morning dead of exposure and hypothermia...frozen to death.

Now, to learn there was no doubt my father had asphyxiated or burned-to-death. What could I do? How could I say: "Well, tough shit Dad. Shit happens. Your life is over and I have mine." I could not.

In the pit of my despair, I resolved to get the answers . . . something must have been learned from my father's suffering and I had to do something much greater for my father than one article in a local paper.

In the weeks of mourning between reading this letter of my father's death and finding my own answer to healing, I was advised by friends and family to "get over it."

Yet, I could not...and would not. I resolved to find out through the Congressional inquiry and any other means what was learned from his suffering, but I also resolved what it was I would do much greater than an article in a local paper. I would write a book that published his letters home.

To those who counseled me away from this course of action my reply was: "No, I'm not going to 'get over' his horrible death. I am determined to 'get through his death'." I told others: "I'm going to do as John Walsh did for his son Adam or the founder of Mothers Against Drunk Driving did for her daughter...something greater in his memory that will help others."

I shared the letter with my mom and my brother. The peace we had fought to restore over the homeless winter was lost to the stress.

I told them I would do the heavy lifting on investigating to learn all I could about the crash; that I would write the book, but could they support my effort in the ways they were capable of?

No! My brother never read the letters again and my mother said this was my "project." In one heated argument she blurted out: "I hate your father! He promised me he would come back from Vietnam and he didn't. You can have the damn letters."

Months passed. The first break came from a tremendous letter I received after locating a pilot who was in the same "hooch" with Dad in Vietnam.

10 Sept 97

Dear Mark:

Last Friday evening I got a call from my wife from our home in Enterprise, Alabama to my brother's house in Wilmington, Delaware, with whom I was visiting for six days. During our phone conversation she mentioned that I had received a letter from "Big John's' son Mark Seeley. I asked Annie to open and read your letter over the phone. Monday morning I was on my way back to Wash, DC, a one hour and thirty two minute trip via AMTRAK from Wilmington Delaware (trains run time, sometime) for a visit to the Vietnam Veterans Memorial to etch your father's name. You may have done this already. I hope this will help your quest for information about your Father.

I and several other pilots arrived in Nam in August 1965 with the 1st Cav. Division. After six months of combat flying with the 1st Cav, several were infuses to other units in Nam. I, along with Maj. Robert Morris was assigned to the 178th Assault Support Helicopter Company, call sign "Boxcars" at Phu Loi RVN, a newly arrived CH-47 Chinook unit which deployed from Ft. Benning, GA. Your father was the platoon leader of the 2nd flight platoon. I was a "peter pilot" assigned to the 1st flight platoon, our Platoon leader was Cpt. Meihoffer. Due to platoon integrity, I never had the opportunity to fly with your father.

However, I did share a "GP Medium Tent" with your father and four other pilots, all slept on a GI issue cot and air mattress w/sleeping bag and insect net hanging above the cot to protect us from one thousand varieties of insects that found their way into our tent. We also shared a fridge which was well-stocked with TOURBERG beer, a Danish beer brewed in Malaysia for her Majesties troops. A cold beer always set well after a long hot, dusty day of flying.. Your father was a tall man. I do recall his long legs sticking out well beyond the cot and insect net. I am certain the bugs had a great time nipping at his toes. We all had stories to swap after a day of flying while sipping our beer. Your father had us all rolling on the floor with his humor on several occasions. This camaraderie I will cherish always.

I do recall June 27, 1966 the day your father and (Josh) CW-2 John R. Logan were involved in a humanitarian type mission hauling captured VC rice to a central point where the rice was distributed to the local Vietnamese people. Something to ponder Mark- your father not only died in service to his country-he also died feeding the hungry. Some gave some-" 'Big John' gave it All"

Please Mark-send a reprint of "Angel, I Write These Things."

Sincerely,

Dennis

In the fall of 1997 I moved from the third-floor apartment at Community House. My stubborn advocacy on behalf of the homeless people in the two floors beneath me had caused strains with the management. It was time to go from this single-room occupancy apartment my homeless writings had gotten me two and-a-half years earlier.

However, by moving I had isolated myself from others. Instead of thirty-nine other single-room residents to befriend and a communal smoking yard used by all the shelter's residents I was alone. Alone with thoughts of father's final moments; alone with a particular recurring, horrific dream set in motion by a letter I received from the pathfinder with Dad's Vietnam helicopter unit who had "Hooked" the web-master up with the surviving pilot's address. In his letter he wrote:

August 21, 1997

...You do not know John was not put out of his misery on the spot by one of the grunts or crewmen who were there. These things most certainly did happen and when they did everyone looked the other way. It had to be that way or someone could have been brought up on murder charges regardless of the circumstances. There were a lot of unwritten understandings between men who were comrades and might be present at one another's death or worse a no-recovery injury.

Of course, between a choice of being shot-to-death or burning-to-death, most would choose the former. In this recurring dream I was a five year old suddenly transported to the scene that day. In the dream, I am standing in front of a burning helicopter. I can see him and I am trying to hold and steady a gun in my small hands so I can shoot my father.

No answers came from the Congressional Inquiry either. When I had decided to initiate the Congressional Inquiry it only made sense to pursue it through the Senator's office because of that internship I'd served in 1982 as a college sophomore majoring in political science and he was a first-term Congressman. What I hadn't taken stock of was the much more recent homelessness of 1994 homelessness may have diminished me in their eyes. Secondly, the staffer who handled it did so without any vigor. He was burned out after years in the job and ultimately resigned the post within a year.

Initially, through my new upstairs neighbor at my apartment and then through use of the public library's computers I found the salve...the only thing to staunch my emotional bleeding over how Dad died. After that tremendous letter from the "hoochmate" I found the only antidote was finding those who served with my father at any point in his military career.

I found an invaluable clearinghouse-VHFCN.ORG...the Vietnam Helicopter Flight Crew Network. On one page were links to active web-sites for Vietnam helicopter units So, I spent countless hours posting the same message in the guest books of these helicopter unit web-sites that said: 'if you knew or served with Captain John Seeley please e-mail me at: markseeley@.....com'

By the spring of 1998 I was getting probably an average of one e-mail a week from men who had served with my father. Also, e-mail condolences from Vietnam veterans from all years of service. The most moving was from a Nashville musician who e-mailed he would not be alive today if it were not for the helicopter pilots. As I scrolled down the e-mail a photo gradually appeared showing him sitting at his piano in a wheelchair. He had no legs. Obviously, he had sacrificed them in service to our country, but revered helicopter pilots for getting him to an aid station in time to save his life.

The VHFCN web-site had a "chat room" where Vietnam pilots would gather at a specific time each evening. They welcomed me in. My sign in name was BJS as an acronym for "Big John's Son". From these pilots I learned so much, but what I remember with fondness was just how quickly these pilots could ferret out Vietnam wanna-be's. Any new sign-in was asked: "When did you serve? Which Corps (region)? What unit? What years?" Often these "wanna-be's" had no answers. Then, they would resort to claiming they flew black psych-ops and couldn't reveal anything. They were then shunned or shamed out of the "chat room" within minutes.

From these pilots I learned how to get the Accident Board report of my father's crash. Disgusted with the glacial pace of the Congressional Inquiry, I sent a certified letter myself asking for the report as John Seeley's youngest son. I requested the report in April 1998 and received it in July of 1998.

It's a good thing I was attending the reunion of his unit...the 178th Assault Support Helicopter Company call sign: "Boxcars: in August of 1998 at Fort Rucker, Alabama. For I was thrown underwater again with sorrow from its heavily redacted pages that did, however, share the autopsy report with 4th degree burns over 100% of body surface and cause of death listed as 'incineration with possible asphyxiation.'

In a later chapter I'll recount not only what it was like to attend this reunion but two more in 2000 and 2003, but for now its enough to say friends-and, yes-family told me I was a much healthier person after I returned from that 178th Boxcar reunion. I met the surviving pilot and at least six other men who served with Dad in 1966.

Home from this reunion I was renewed and better able to cope with this Accident report. What had caused the crash? The Army, in their stupid and paranoid reasoning, redacted 80% of the contents including the Board's conclusions as to what caused it. So, in Army brat fashion I had to soldier on. The cause could have been mechanical failure, weight overload, small-arms fire from the Viet Cong, or a failure to account for temperature change.

The only possible avenue for answers was to find the witnesses. In the report I had all of the witness statements. The only thing blacked out was their service numbers. I had their full names.

Yes, I had the horror of the autopsy report, but I had confirmed my suspicions. I had been dead-on correct in the TV story. The last two sentences of the surviving pilot's witness statement closed with: "I believe I could have saved Captain Seeley if I had a survival knife strapped to my hip or an axe."

In 1996 I saw the movie "Courage Under Fire" starring Denzel Washington and Meg Ryan: a fictional movie about an investigation into whether a Desert Strom female helicopter pilot should be the first Medal of Honor recipient. Denzel Washington plays the officer tasked with investigating whether Meg Ryan's character, the female Army Captain helicopter pilot, should receive the nation's highest honor.

Well, I wrote a rough draft to this book in 2004 and watched the close of that movie three times over the month-long leave of absence my employer granted me to work on the rough draft. Why?

In the movie's close Denzel Washington's character is submitting his final report to his superior. In a masterful acting job Denzel Washington fights back the hint of tears in his eyes as he tells his superior: "We've got to tell the cold hard truth or we disrespect her and all those who've given their lives for this country."

Oh, how I wish this book were a work of fiction. Male life expectancy is 78 now…except for the cold, hard truths you will read of in the next chapter I could be sitting down now with my Army Captain helicopter pilot father.

Captain John S. Seeley's death could have been avoided, but to borrow military parlance the mission that killed my Dad was FUBAR… Fucked Up Beyond Any Recognition.

Yet, just as Denzel Washington states in COURAGE UNDER FIRE I owe my father the 'cold, hard truth.'

Chapter 6- "Exempt From Disclosure"

When John Kennedy Jr's plane went down off of Martha's Vineyard the National Transportation Safety Board did not investigate the crash and then deny the public the facts with this proviso: N.T.S.B has redacted major portions of the report to "preserve the integrity of the safety investigation process..." and are "exempt from disclosure so that individuals involved may freely and openly provide uninhibited opinions and recommendations..." Yet, this is the sad logic used in the letter I received in July 1998 that accompanied the Accident Board Report into my father's death with the Accident Board's conclusions blacked-out.

Yet, it's been over 42 years since my father's Chinook went down and collapsed our family into a grief carried in some measure each day by my mother, brother, and I.

I did not mean to burden my brother with the certainty the letters he cannot bear to even read 10% of came from a father whose fate was just like the Blackwater employees whose charred corpses were hung from that bridge in Fallujah, Iraq.

So, just what was learned from my father's physical and psychological suffering? In civilian life people go to prison and lawsuits clog the court system when corporate or personal mistakes cause loss of life.

Yet, to view the conundrum of war in a cynical vein is to argue military officers find ways to get their men killed in pursuit of a victory that is not assured. From the tactics of Union General Ulysses Grant in the Civil War to the Chinese crossing the Yalu River in the Korean War history is replete with examples. Yet, General Patton said: "I don't want you men to die for our country, but get the enemy's dumb bastards to die for theirs."

The U.S. Army did succeed in getting my father killed, but from faulty seat design; the "Iron Maiden" armor sheath limiting his mobility; the engineers blowing out a PZ of insufficient size and an OPS officer whose desire to see a mission completed led to him taunting the officer-on-the-scene, my father, that he and the other pilot might not have the "skill" to complete the mission and the surviving pilot failing to ask how his stick-buddy was before making his hasty exit and then asking Dad how he was from the outside and unable to get back in and free my father's legs…for Dad was not wounded; his feet were entangled in the wreckage.

The Air Force bombed the site after the crash to deny the supplies left in that "stinking jungle" to use my mother's words. Why couldn't that have been done to begin with? One of the two Huey pilots flying light fire support watched helplessly from 300 feet as the Chinook failed to clear the final 20 feet of 70 foot tall trees.

The Huey Captain I located in 1999 said: "Mark, I consulted on the periphery of mid-1980's documentary. The top Army boot on-the-ground in Vietnam in 1966 was General Westmoreland. He was asked in hindsight if he would change anything about his approach/execution if he could and he said, "Maybe the body count system."

He continued the analytical statement that military men are capable of tapping into; a voice distanced from the import and hurt of their words on a son's weight overloaded heart; "Your father died for the same illogic. It wasn't enough for him to record in notepad the number of tin sheets, bicycles, pots & pans and come back to base with it. The VC material had to be, like a VC corpse-produced-to meet mission requirements."

Now, my own 'mission requirements' demanded I do what I struggled with over the past decade: excise my heart from the facts, but just how to do that evades me still. How could I look the page in the Accident Board report with the fact the blood in his vital organs was listed as coagulated, a head wound listed as post-mortem, and nothing that could bring any solace at all.

In 2001 I located a Sergeant with the 1st Infantry B/2/16 that loaded the supplies. I had his witness statement in front of me. When he answered the phone I gave a very brief description of the KIA date and the fact it was a Chinook crash. I identified myself as the pilot's son. Yet, he did not know how much I knew. He said "you mean the crash where the pilot crashed and burned?" He followed this with a question: "You did not have an open casket funeral, did you?"

I replied that my mother did not allow my brother and I to attend the funeral, but I knew it wasn't an open casket funeral.

He then said: "That's good because I was part of the team that recovered his body."

We talked a little, but he told me he knew where another Sergeant was that witnessed the crash and gave me the man's phone number.

I wasn't oblivious to the fact these calls could be taxing for these veterans: to drop into their lives suddenly via a phone call to ask questions about a memory they might otherwise not prefer to remember. Thus, I hesitated to call this other Sergeant. What more could be learned?

I'd learned in this research that I had to pursue every avenue because there always seemed to be something that I could learn.

I was very glad I did place that call because this other Sergeant told me the rice that was burned with the bladder of contaminated JP-4 was 'tax rice'.

"Tax rice?" I replied.

"Yeah, it was State side rice...as we cut the bags open the State in the U.S. where it was from was listed on the bags. The VC would collect the rice from villages sympathetic to the "liberation" of South Vietnam to feed the VC their soldiers rodent-like existence; those villages supporting the South Vietnamese would have the village leader threatened as the VC confiscated the rice by force as the village's "tax" to liberate South Vietnam from democracy."

The process of discovery of the truth of what happened that day was not clean and orderly. Had the Army not been paranoid and redacted so much of the report my quest would have been easier.

In 2003 I thought I had a breakthrough when I found the officer who wrote the Accident Board Report. He thought it was horseshit that the Army had redacted 80% of the report. So, I sent him a copy, but too many years had passed. He could not remember what was in the blacked-out pages. He knew where another board member was and forwarded the report to him. Same result. Again, too many years had passed.

The crash of "Boxcar 162" could have been caused by one of many causes: Was it overloaded? Was it brought down by VC small-arms fire? Did my father and the A/C Logan fail to account for increased temperature and humidity between 9 a.m. and 3 p.m. which were the times the CH-47 lifted off with full loads?

Without the Board's conclusions to examine I was left with trying to locate the witnesses. Some were found easily; others took years. Three have never been located.

In most instances not much more was learned about the crash itself for they had offered what they knew in their witness statements in the first 9 days after the crash. Yet, as the KIA pilot's son it was compelling to just be actually speaking to the men who saw my father in the last hours of his life.

When Dad decided to leave with a half-load around noon, he went down in the jungle to advise the Infantry Captain whose men were loading the captured VC tin sheets, bicycles, and pots & pans into the CH-47. Dad told him he was not risking a $1 million dollar Chinook and his crew for VC junk.

Ironically, I located him after a Google search took me to the web-site of an elementary school class project. A student wrote of the mayor visiting and that he had been a 'solder' in Vietnam. As this book is written, this Infantry Captain is still the mayor of a major Western U.S. city. When I did not get a response to my initial request I located his home phone number. He was not home for he was attending a National Conference of Mayors event in Washington D.C.

His wife enjoined me to not e-mail again if I did not get a response. She said: "Since my husband is in politics he lets the public know he is a veteran who served his country proudly, but he never talks about Vietnam in private."

I spoke to a close friend whose father-Raymond Tudor-was a retired transport pilot. His father had dropped paratroopers into Operation Market-Garden in WWII. He urged me to not pursue it further if the Infantry Captain did not respond. As I waited days and days I began to lose hope. Then, weeks after the conversation with the wife, I finally received his e-mail that emphasized everyone was nervous and a confirmation he knew of my father's horrific manner of dying when he wrote:

> Mark, as I recall that time, a long time ago...as so often was the case, there were reports of enemy activity and most of my battalion, 1st Bn, 16th Inf. was put in by choppers at several different locations....my company sort of wandered into this large supply complex...we were getting sporadic contact and kept pursuing and all of sudden we were into a huge and I do mean huge complex....supplies...rice, bikes, tin, food, med supplies. I think it was a major resupply complex. For several days we tried to patrol and determine the actual size and every day we ran into the enemy...at night we closed back into a defensive position and our ambush patrols and listening posts reported hearing movement. And what seemed to be people loading supplies and moving them out...we used Artillery but it was a very large area...I and others were sure they were coming in at night and taking weapons and ammo out...never proven. I think I recall that other supply items were taken out to villages in the area...the decision to fly the stuff out was made very high up...I had many general officers visit...I don't recall the tin numbers change unless it made sense....I don't believe, in my mind, that it was intended to deceive. Wish I could recall more of my conversations with your Dad...he was a large guy. None of us were "Fat", and his concern for his crew and chopper was evident and his nervousness was not unusual. Hell, I was nervous. The VC were trying to find us by lobbing mortar and firing rounds, hoping we would ID our location...we did not...your Dad did sit with me and talked for some time...about what was happening and what we had found...I am sure.

> Mark, I pray in my soul that your Dad didn't suffer and that his body was able to shut down so he felt little pain. He was a brave man who cared for his troops and is deserving of our respect and honor...Your book is a great tribute to your Dad, his service and memory and all our comrades in arms who gave their lives for what we were told was a just cause...I am proud of your Dad and all Vietnam vets. We served proudly, we didn't lose that war. Spineless politicians lost that war. Hope this is helpful.

> God bless you and your Mom.

Finding the witnesses took patience and perseverance. For example, it took five years to find the flight engineer of Boxcar 162. I called many phone numbers in Southern states from doing basic whitepages.com searches. His name was neither common nor uncommon, but enough potential matches that I made numerous calls. All to no avail. Most of these searches were in the years of 1998-2000. Oddly, a similar search in 2003 revealed his number. Again, not much was added to my knowledge of the day's events except he finally gave me something to laugh about regarding what happened that day. He said the gunner did not participate when Dad asked the crew, as they ate C-rations, whether he should call base and attempt to cancel as they re-fueled at Lai Khe. The gunner negotiated with a villager and bought the woman's pig. I guess he planned on a nice bacon breakfast back at base the next morning. Lucky for the pig that it fought off his purchase for as the Ch-47 fired up the rotors the pig bit the gunner's hand and ran off and the flight engineer told the gunner there was no time for the gunner to recover his investment for the back ramp was going up "NOW."

My father's date with death and this book would not exist if either the Operations Officer had permitted my father to scrub the mission or, very possibly, if the surviving pilot had asked my father his condition before exiting the burning chopper The "Iron Maiden" armor sheath limited my father's mobility. Since his feet were entangled in the throttles Dad could not move his feet to free his torso; he could not move his torso to free his feet because he was buckled into the "Iron Maiden."

The surviving pilot's letter in 1997 to the HELI-VETS web-master differed little from his sworn written statement to the Accident Board. Yet, another mistake from early in the war sealed my father's fate and left the surviving pilot with a hefty amount of "survivor's guilt" until his death in December 2006 at age 78 from leukemia. In the surviving pilot's three-paged single-space typed statement to the Accident Board on July 5, 1966 he concluded with: "I believe if I had a survival knife strapped to my hip or an axe I could have saved the Captain."

The Accident Board could have limited its inquiry into the crash itself, but also chose to examine my father's attempt to cancel the mission. Finding the Major who wrote the report in 2002 had been a wash in terms of finding out the Board's conclusions, but did allow me to ask him something that had puzzled me since I'd first read through the report four years earlier.

The witness statements were very thorough. The crew chief whom the surviving pilot ran into in a standby room in 1967 at 'Mother Rucker' was interviewed at a Saigon hospital on June 28, 1966 by the 178th's Flight Surgeon and Battalion Safety Officer. Due to the severity of his burns he was mede-vaced to Brooke Army Hospital in San Antonio, Texas on June 29, 1966. He had been administered a tracheotomy and was unable to speak. He nodded "yes" or "no" answers to 7 questions. Then these officers listed their titles and signed their signatures that they had witnessed the burned crew chief's yes or no nods of the head.

Two witnesses to the conversation between the 178th's Operations Officer and my father submitted sworn statements to the Board as to what they heard of the conversation. I've never found Mr. Golumb or Mr. Holterhoff.

Yet, there is no statement from the Operations Officer. Why? The Accident Board President is a wonderful man who has helped as much is possible. Yet, in our conversations I did pose this cynical theory as to why the Operations Officer never made a witness statement. Over drinks at the Officer Club the Board President said: "Hey, I've got two statements from your clerks that support your position so I won't have you go under oath in a written statement…you're an Army Major and so am I. For your military records to include you sent a pilot back into a horrific death is not something anyone wants in their record. And here's a toast to the future of our Army careers."

Technically, the two clerks who have never been located could have avoided perjuring themselves in their witness statements by claiming permission to cancel was granted. Remember, the surviving pilot had written in his 1997 letter the Operations Officer said: "If you two don't have the skills, I'll send someone else in."

Remember that Captain John Seeley fought to get back to Vietnam so another pilot would not be put in Harm's Way to complete his one-year tour of duty in Vietnam. Thus, when my father was told he could cancel his mission, but told another pilot would be sent in Dad felt he had not been given a choice. Dad's code of duty…honor…country meant he had to complete his tour…and, of course, complete missions without someone else being sent in to do what he had been assigned. The Operations officer gave permission for John Seeley and his crew to cancel their mission, but the mission itself would be completed.

Ultimately, the Army did agree with Cpt. John Seeley that the captured tin sheets, bicycles, and post and pans were not worth the risk, but only after my father gave his life to prove the point: for, as you know, the Air Force bombed the site to deny the enemy the remaining supplies.

As you will read later I attended three re-unions of my father's Vietnam CH-47 unit...the 178th "Boxcars." The surviving pilot was at each one. He was a very likable man with a gregarious and out-going personality. Though I had questions about some of his accounts I grew protective of him.

Thus, it was jarring when I finally located the medic who made a final rescue attempt after pulling the surviving pilot away from the wreckage. He and a Rifleman had come upon the scene, but the Rifleman had been KIA in September 1966.

From a posting in the Internet site guestbook of C/2nd/16 I had gotten many false leads. The medic's name is a fairly common one. Then, just a month after returning from the 2003 178th Boxcar reunion a soldier said he had an old roster for B/2nd/16th of the 1st Infantry. He provided an e-mail address. I e-mailed a brief sketch of the crash facts. His e-mail reply…just hours later…left no doubt this Medic was the last one with my father.

I never told my mother and brother of this medic's witness statement. I had held out my own hope from the surviving pilot's account in his June 27, 1997 letter to the webmaster that my father had succumbed to the smoke, but from this witness statement that hope was torn from me:

June 29, 1966

...when we finished loading, the helicopter took off, it rose almost vertically and started forward. As it moved forward it began to settle back down to the ground. It hit the trees at the far end of the field, where dome trees had been cut down, and crashed, falling on its right hand side. I grabbed my medical bag and ran toward the aircraft. I had to go through some heavy brush and small trees. When I got there I saw a crew member, a PFC or SP4, he appeared dazed but not badly harmed. I called for a medic. Then I saw a SP6 who appeared to be unharmed. He was standing near the rear of the helicopter. He said that he saw the helicopter was going to crash so he let the ramp down. I left him and went around to the front I had to go around by the tree line because of the fire and I could hear rounds exploding in the helicopter.

In front I saw SP4 Dominguez assisting a man out of the wreckage. It was CWO Logan. I helped him and then looked the officer over. He tried to go back inside the aircraft but I was afraid he might be injured already and do himself more harm. We set him down about twenty yards from the helicopter. Then SP4 Dominguez and I went back to the airplane and tried to breakout the windows to get to the other pilot. We could not pull him out. I called to him, "Captain, if you can hear me say something or move." He moved his foot! We then tried to free his feet from the pedals but we could not. Suddenly flames and smoke just seemed to explode and jump into the front of the helicopter. It didn't seem like a regular explosion, more like gun powder had exploded or something. We had to get away. Then I saw CWO Logan moving again. I went over to try and calm him and keep him still when I got back to the helicopter the Captain was on fire. Dominguez and I put CWO Logan on a stretcher and took him to the CP

In the years since I have explained to people that I had to do this book...that it was my apology for how my father suffered. At times people have nodded a quick acknowledgement when I've said "my Dad burned-to-death alive." When it seems they are not registering the import of that fact, I've asked them to close their eyes and imagine their parents-living or dead- burning to death...to visualize this for two minutes. Most decline this hypothetical, but it's a fact I carried alone for years.

In the fall of 2003 I found the medic who wrote the witness statement. I spoke to him that very night I received his e-mail. I described the surviving pilot's letter and he said: "The surviving pilot could not have had the time to do all he claimed he did to save your Dad. I watched the Chinook take off with my Sergeant. When I saw it was going into the trees I began to run toward where I thought it would crash. He didn't have time-I was there pulling him away in just a few minutes."

For the next nine months we exchanged a few e-mails. He retreated from his position on the actions of the surviving pilot stating that combat trauma is something no one but veterans can understand. I was relieved by this because I was protective of the surviving pilot's words because I had met him three times at the 178th Boxcar reunions.

The Moving Wall visited the nearby town of Mountain Home in June of 2004. An unguarded conversation with a WWII veteran prompted me to ask for a month leave-of-absence from work to actually start writing the rough draft of the book. Thinking this Moving Wall Volunteer would offer up a story of his WWII service, I asked why he was volunteering. He pointed to the West Wall and told me his son was on one of the panels…of how he and his wife moved to Canada for years because they had become disillusioned with our country.

Small world. The medic lived only 90 miles away and drove to Boise on business often. We set up a meeting at my local coffee shop the day before the official start of leave-of-absence.

As I waited for his arrival, I had the surviving pilot's 1997 letter to the webmaster and the surviving pilot's witness statement to the Accident Board ready for him. For the next fifteen minutes he read them…at times going back-and-forth between the two.

He then looked up and said: "With all due respect to the surviving pilot; this is not what happened."

Beside the time frame, he turned over a piece of paper and sketched a drawing. He said the surviving pilot's claim of trying to go through "all kinds of bluish smoke and flames" could not have happened because that vertical pane-glass window to the left of father's left-hand seat that was now "the top" was not damaged at all and was fully intact.

A key revelation for the Accident Board could have concluded with "asphyxiation and possible incineration" had they known no smoke was escaping.

Yet, the medic's own statement betrayed such a conclusion for he had yelled "Captain, if you are alive signal me. He moved his foot!"

When he first sat down he said: "Mark, I have three sons. If I had not made it back from Vietnam and someone I served with was asked to help my boys bring closure to my death I can only hope one of my brothers-in-arms would be willing to meet with them. So, I am here though this is not easy for me either."

After the discussion of the surviving pilot we talked about those final moments. Despite what he had written days after the crash that made it sound like my father was conscious and physically responded to a plea for a signal that Dad was alive he said: "Mark, I don't want to be morbid, but when men are dying their bodies can make involuntary, jerking movements. I believe that was the movement I described, but I continued the rescue attempt and had my hand on your father's foot, but he was a big man and I couldn't pull him up."

After that we talked about Vietnam. He told me that civilians could never understand all that men gave over there; of a bond between soldiers that is love…not the love of a man and wife, but in a different way no less strong. The Iraq war was in its infancy, but we shared opinions on that as well.

As the medic walked away to his car I remember thinking his words; his sensitivity; his intelligence mirrored the kind of conversation I'd imagined before having with my own father had he lived. Like my father this veteran was one of America's best. In that I found peace and it gave me resolve for the tough month ahead.

During the writing of the rough draft of the book one more disturbing "fact" was to come to light. I called many of the veterans I had spoken to for permission to use their names in the book. One helicopter pilot with the 178th had sent me an e-mail in 1999 of how the surviving pilot would threaten violence on those who would try to help him in the weeks after the crash by going to the GP-6 medium tent he shared with other pilots and trying to talk to him to help him.

Yet, in contacting this pilot for permission to reprint his e-mail he told me something much more profound. He said the night of the crash he was called to that tent when someone ran up and told him: "Can you come to our tent…Josh waved us out of the tent with a 45 and is threatening to kill himself."

This pilot said from the lip of the tent he talked him out of it reminding him he had a wife at home that loved him and buddies that cared for him and would help him.

This claim threw me into a three-day funk. Although I was taking medications for my manic-depression they couldn't stop the depression that ensued. I knew I had to call the surviving pilot with two questions. First, the medic had told me that his version of events could not have happened. Second, "Did he wave everyone out of his tent the night of the crash threatening suicide?"

I made this call reluctantly and he said: "You can take it to the bank that what I said I did, I did. And No! I've never been suicidal."

So, throughout the years of research every hope of a "soft landing" for my emotions on my father's final moments seemed to be torn away. Was the medic's words days after the crash the truth or was it what he told me in a meeting where he had said he hoped I could gain closure. I don't know and will never know.

What is certain is a memo sent to all levels of command from November 1966. At each of the three 178th reunions I took this Accident Board Report along...just in case. The only part I ever took out was the memo summarized below and I shared it only with the surviving pilot. Its contents prove my father's five to ten minutes of suffering and the anguish the surviving pilot carried all his life until his burial in Arlington amongst his fellow heroes in April of 2007 was not in vain. Both John Seeley and John Logan and their crew contributed greatly to the safety of Army Aviation when Boxcar 162 went down in that VC-infested jungle on 6-27-66.

Accident Board memo summarized.

The memo was dated November 4, 1966 and sent to the Commander in Chief, U.S. Army Pacific; as well as the Commanding Generals of the U.S. Army, Vietnam and the 1st Aviation Brigade. Copies also went to the Commanding Officers of the 12th Aviation Group and the 11th Aviation Battalion.

The reviewing official, Colonel George Handley, wrote in a final report dated 4 Nov 1966

1. Concur with the findings and recommendations of the accident investigation board as amended by the reviewing official.
2. Headquarters, USARV Aviation Pamphlet dated October 66 indicates the "Go-No-Go" placards and instructions are now available in Vietnam.
3. The comments relating to the crashworthiness of the seats with armor protection have been noted. Action has been taken to investigate these

reported deficiencies in the seat installed in the "Iron Maiden" configuration. Xxxxxxxxxxxxxxxxxxxxxxxxxxxxxxxxxxxx. [Two lines blacked out with the justification "Analysis" marked next to this redaction.]

4. AVCOM has awarded a contract to National Waterlift Company for the development of a gross weight/center-of-gravity indicator for the CH-47A helicopter. USAAvaTBd will conduct service testing in early 1967.

5. The comments of the reviewing official in paragraph 5 in regard to individual survival equipment have been noted. TA 8-100 presently authorizes the PSK-2 survival kit. The "Rocket Jet" survival kit requested by RVN through an Expedited Non-Standard Urgent Requirement for Equipment (ENSURE) message to DA is in the procurement stage. It is estimated first shipments of the "Rocket Jet" kit should be ready in April 1967.

6. USABAAR is continuously monitoring and endeavoring to expedite the development of crash resistant fuel cells and emulsified fuels in order to reduce the occurrence of post-crash fires.

Prior to the crash of Boxcar 162, Boeing Corporation, the manufacturer of the CH-47 had been developing a placard for the pilots to use which will "permit the aviator to determine performance capabilities when operating under conditions of high altitude and high ambient temperatures that impose power limits." This memo confirms the Army did get these placards to units in Vietnam.

Yet, I believe my father's greatest contribution to the safety of Army Aviation came with the removal of the "Iron Maiden" armor sheath. I believe my father's death-by-incineration received great attention back at the manufacturer. The Army can redact, deny, and obfuscate as much as they wish to, but no one will deter me from the belief what was learned from his death was some percentage of the reason Boeing removed the "Iron Maiden."

I confirmed with a 147th "Hillclimber" pilot who flew with the surviving pilot of Dad's crash after "Josh" transferred to Vung Tau that the "Iron Maiden" armor sheath was removed and with the B model the pilots wore an armor vest they called "chicken plates."

My father was a positive and forward-looking husband, father, and pilot. In death he contributed to the safety of Army Aviation. His death underscores the very thin line that separates our Vietnam veterans from their brothers-on-the-Wall. John Logan told me that Dad boarded Boxcar 162 first and took the left-hand seat... had Dad chosen the right-hand seat then it could have well been John Logan on the Vietnam Wall.

The rest of this proud son's journey is a return to the celebration of the life of John Seeley. Yes, the next chapter is sorrowful for it, in part, recounts the grief of those who served with "Big John" and mourned his loss in letters to my mother, but the depth of their grief is best read as their affection, and yes, love, for my Dad. For without love there is no sorrow.

Chapter 7- "We Share in Your Sorrow"

(From Jerry Ziegler)

July 15, 1966

Dear Alice, Doug, and Mark

Sally sent your address as I wanted you to know how very much we share in your sorrow. Our prayer is that despite John's death you and the boys will find happiness in life. I know that this was John's constant ambition. In a letter he sent to me in May one phrase in particular hit home. It was so typical of John. He was talking of Alaska when he said "looking back on these happy kids with lots of noise reminds me of all the things worthwhile in our lives." Here, to me is the goal he lived for.

This year in Viet Nam has been a series of revelations for me, not many of them pleasant. But when the outlook is the bleakest, one thing that has kept me going has been the example of a few dedicated men who are willing to do a job that needs to be done despite the obstacles. I've always counted John as one of these men. It was in the service of this dedication that he gave his life for.

I hope that we'll be able to see each other in December, Alice I know how much Sally is counting on it. Whatever happens please keep in touch, and don't hesitate to let us know if there is ever any way we can help out. Our prayers are always with you.   Love, Jerry

(From Pat Moss)

22 July 1966

Dear Alice:

I'm writing in an effort to express my deepest sympathy over John's very untimely death.

As you know, I've known John for a long time-seven years to be exact and will hold many memories of him.

In the time I've known him, he has always had a very high sense of responsibility for his family. He spoke often of his feelings for you and the two boys. One of his hardest times was when he first came to Korea in 1961. He took it very hard that he had to be separated from you. Here, he was in the midst of preparing justification to be given leave to visit you in Hawaii. If this information is any consolation to you, I am sorry that I've waited so long to set it down on paper.

I know that you will be wanting to know John's feeling for his presence in this place called VietNam. He expressed many times his feeling that this was a nasty little war and he wanted no part of it; yet, since it had to be done, he preferred to do it here rather at a time and place which would expose his family to the face of war. I flew with John on his first mission after he came back from Japan and he stated that he had fought to get back in order that he would complete a tour here as soon as possible and that he could be of some help in aiding the war effort here rather than have a new pilot join the unit. John was perfectly capable of performing his job of actually flying the aircraft and making decisions in view of the overall requirements. Due to this capability, he chose to continue a mission of evacuating captured enemy war materials. As a result of his personal decision he hoped to achieve total evacuation and deny the enemy access to the material; however, the result ended in John losing his life for a cause he believed in.

As the Unit Administrative officer, I processed all of the initial reports on John. This has caused me to withdraw each time I have wanted to write. I have started to several times but could not finish. So after making excuses, I'll apologize again for delaying to write you. Again, please accept my sympathy in your grief, and, please, if there is any way I can help you at any time do not hesitate to write.   Sincerely, Pat

(From Major Shields)

1 Aug 1966
Phu Loi, RVN

Dear Mrs. Seeley,

I wish I could answer all your questions. There are many questions for which a board of officers have to answer if an answer is possible. The Accident Board Report has not yet submitted an approved report although it appears to be a combat loss rather than an aircraft accident. The site of the crash was in an area controlled by the Viet Cong and after the evacuation of the aircraft occupants, the area could not be secured without the risk of greater loss of life.

Since the Accident Board has not yet determined the cause of the crash, I can only tell you what I heard from the survivors. This is unofficial and hearsay only.
This is the same information I sent to Captain Charles H. Frady who wrote me two weeks ago.

John and "Josh" Logan were on mission to remove captured V.C. material from a "hot" area. They flew three sorties from the same area and on the fourth take-off, the CH-47 lost rotor spin and settled into tall trees. After falling through the trees, the CH-47 landed on the right side.

"Josh" was temporarily blinded but managed to crawl through the broken Plexiglass. He said that John's seat had broken loose and that John appeared to be paralyzed. "Josh worked to get John out but John made absolutely no movements to help. He spoke only one phrase to say he couldn't move and then was evidently unconscious or dead. Josh made every effort to help for five or ten minutes with no response or movement from John. An explosion blew Josh away from the aircraft inflicting wounds which have not yet healed. Infantry arrived on the scene and physically restrained anyone from approaching the wreckage. John and "Josh" were classmates in flight school as was Pat Moss in this unit. Josh still has nightmares and blames himself for not being able to do more. I'm sure that Josh did all that was humanely possible to extricate his buddy who was most certainly dead. The Accident Report and autopsy have not been released but I'm sure John's death was painless based on the testimony of the witnesses.

The Flight Engineer, George Luster, escaped the crash only to be severely wounded last week by a VC bomb attack in Vung Tau. The crew chief was severely burned and is now at Brooke Army Medical Center in San Antonio, Texas.

I understand your bitterness about John dieing in a "stinking" country but he had compassion for and more for some of the crippled, twisted little kids who are innocent victims of this war against terrorists and sadists. He could picture you and your boys in this situation as I can picture Joan and my boys. We had discussed it often Its a dirty war and we don't know what the outcome will be. I believe that John died doing what he wanted to do and believed in. We all loved him as buddies and as a combat pilot sharing a special bond of comradeship. The love of a man for a woman is far more intimate and special than what a so-called rugged aviator is supposed to feel for a good buddy. We all feel deeply in our own way and we all miss "Big John."

Please write again if you can. After we get over the shock I'm sure that all our guys can recount many stories of John's fun side that you and the boys may not have heard. I'd like to tell your boys what a big man John really was.

If I should survive this tour I'd feel privileged to see you and the boys on my way home next February. Enclosed are some pictures of the memorial service held here at Phu Loi. I suppose that tears are not appropriate on an aviator's cheeks but I saw some.
Please write.   With love, Roger Shields

(From Pat Moss)

11 August 1966

Hello Alice

Your letter came today so I will make time to answer it.

We have been in a lull for the past two or three days but tomorrow the 173 Abn Bgd is off for another operation and we are committed heavily in support of them.

I'll try to answer your questions as you asked them to the best of my ability. Major Shields has not had the time to write a decent letter. We have some unique problems here in this Unit and he carries them all. We are trying to ship him out on R & R but so far he has not gone.

John "Josh" Logan was with John as were the Flight Engineer the crew chief and the gunner. John is O.K. He was burned, scratched, cut and bruised, but is now flying again. He is still feeling very badly about the crash and is assigned with a responsible person. He may or may not write to you. He constantly talks about writing but then tapers off. You can contact him using the same address I have. The Flight Engineer was all cut up but is O.K. now. The Crew Chief is at Brooke Army Hospital in San Antonio Texas. This is the burn center. He is totally blinded and cannot use his hands. The gunner was burned on both hands but is O.K. now.

The crash happened due to loss of rotor spin and subsequently went into the trees. The loss of RPM was due to an over weight condition. The load was such that it was impossible to estimate the weight. The Accident Board Report proved that the stack of tin could have doubled in weight but not reflect in increased height as it compressed as more was stacked on. The board also brought out that a power check could not be made before take off due to debris in the area. All in all, it was a situation which we have daily over here and the way it is handled is up to the individual pilot on the spot at the moment. According to Josh it if were to be done over again; the same decisions would probably be made. No, there was no fuel being carried. Fire was from the fuel actually in the aircraft. As you know, the fire cells run up both sides of the aircraft so that when there is fire, it is all over instantly. The aircraft did explode after 2-3 minutes. I cannot say that John was killed instantly; however, the autopsy reports shows that he had a large head concussion from which he could not have survived. As for suffering from fire; it is believed that he did not due to the head injury.

It is a terrible thing to say that we must lose people to learn but the Chinook is a new aircraft with capabilities and limitations that even the engineers are still worrying about. One contributing factor is that the armor plating which wraps around us so nicely may have been too heavy for the seat and come free allowing the head injury. All of this under study back at the Board at Rucker and the manufacturer. John was very proud to be flying the machine and I believe that he would join me in saying that it is the greatest even though we must still learn about it.

I'm getting off track here. I hope I have written some of what you asked to your satisfaction.

We are thinking of naming our first BOQ here in honor of John. It would be called "Seeley Hall." We must have your permission first. If you feel that you would wish John memorialized this way could you give us statement of permission. It can be in your own words but on a separate piece of paper in order that it can be entered to the records.

Don't let me present a false picture, however, I may never see a permanent BOQ here. It will all depend on what plans are followed through on.

Before I write a book I will close by saying again if I can help please feel free to say so.   Sincerely, Pat

(From Major Roger Shields)

27 Aug 66

Dear Alice:

It's obvious that I'm a terrible correspondent and I do apologize.

I share your concern with Josh Logan but I sincerely feel that a letter from you to him at this time would only aggravate his condition. He went off the deep end tonight, got drunk, and broke another pilot's leg. I intend to discuss Josh at length with the flight surgeon tomorrow. If Doc feels that a letter from you would help, then I'll let you know immediately. Again, I'm amazed and gratified over your concern. I think that a lesser person than yourself might be most bitter.

Our unit, the 178th, had been involved in some rough battles lately and we've had several more wounded. We were honored today by a decoration of the battalion by the commander of the 3rd Vietnamese Corps. We received the Vietnamese Cross of Gallantry and I'll see that your boys receive it in addition to John's other hard-won decorations I don't recall whether I told you that John had been recommended for the Distinguished Flying Cross. No one in the 178th has ever received one- we'd be proud to hear that it was awarded to you for John's heroism.

I have no other news for now. If your boys are interested, I'd be pleased to send them some pictures of the 178th in action.

Please write when you can.

Roger Shields

(A final letter from Roger Shields)

15 Sep 66
Phu Loi, RVN

Dear Alice:

By the time you return from Bangkok, I hope to have a package assembled with remembrances of the "fighting 178th" to include pictures and our new unit patch.

I had to ground Josh for a week. He was in bad shape. Doc finally cleared him for flight and he is in much better shape. John's death hit him very hard and he retreated to the bottle for a long time.

Time has a way of ameliorating the hurt and Josh is back on the job. I think that Josh could now appreciate a letter from you. He does need reassurance which I've tried to give him. The poor guy will have nightmares for a long time. We love you for your unselfish concern. We "tough guys" are really not so tough as we pretend. The most hard-bitten sergeant in the 178th who worked for "Big John" as Motor Sergeant kept a straight face when I told him what happened but tears rolled down his straight face. I guess that we're all big bad guys fighting a nasty war but you gals at home know that most of us are scared little boys trying to do a job.

Someday this mess will end and there will be no more young widows and little kids who don't understand what happened to their "daddy". How do you explain it? I can't.

Alice, I wish you well and hope that you can relax and have a good time in Bangkok. Regrets and memories aside, life continues.

Speaking for the 178th we all love you and I'll try to see you on my way home.

Love, Rog

P.S. My name is not Maj; its Rog, Ok?

A letter to Dad's father from high school buddy & fellow pilot Chuck Frady regarding Mom's impending visit to Bangkok and up to Udorn, Thailand where "Chuck" Frady was flying for Air America.

30 Sept 1966

Dear Dad & Ruth

Thanks ever so much for the letter you sent. I shall keep it and refer to it when I need strength during the years to come.

We leave by auto early in the morning to pick up Alice in Bangkok. We'll be at the airport when she arrives and already have reservations at a five hotel in the city. We will wine and dine Alice and encourage her to relax. After a couple of days of sight seeing we will bring her up here to relax even more.

I realize Alice is searching for something- possibly a link with John, and I think the very act of coming to our location and its proximity to Viet Nam will help her to call to John and possibly hear him." I've come as close as the mountains will permit and I can feel your last presence, I can go home now." We will try to get her on the right road.

By the way, there will be no expenses for Alice whatsoever and I will take care of her ticket for I feel the future of her and those boys will call for wise budget management. You can rest assured I will never let them go without.

It's a selfish thing to earn good money and want to help loved ones but I am giving in to it for I've never been able to indulge myself on this score.

You know Stu, I too remember John as a lad when we were forming ourselves into the rather complex and inward searching people we turned out to be. We understood each other better than ourselves.

Each day as I fly over Laos and look down into the dense jungle and wonder how many rifles are pointed at me waiting for me to come lower so they can put a round in me. I fly in fear as do we all. My fear is partly for self but mostly for my loved ones. In John's last letter to me, he expressed this fear and my answer can only be expressed now "relax John, I'm going to watch over them as you would mine."

Time to ring off and take my brood swimming. Include us in your prayers and thoughts.   Love-Chuck and Pat

(Letter from surviving pilot)

9 Nov 66 Wednesday
Vung Tau

Dear Alice:

Please forgive me for not writing much sooner. I always said to myself that I will write to Alice tomorrow. Tomorrow it was the same. I don't really have an excuse. Maybe I thought it would only bring the tragedy back to your mind. I realize that you can never forget it, so here I am writing.

I'm glad you wrote to me Alice. I sure did appreciate your letter. I received it on my return from Taipei, Taiwan. I got a second R&R the C.O. recommended that I get another one. Bit of therapy, I guess. I had been drinking a good bit. I went to bed half loaded every night. On two occasions when I was half loaded the name of "Big John" came up. I ended up crying. I'm a little too old to cry I guess so the C.O. had me see the Flight Surgeon. He put me on pills and no booze for a few weeks. I thought I was O.K. but I had to humor him. I drink now but not like back in July and August. Does it seem silly for a grown man to cry over the loss of a good friend? I felt very close to John. I know how you must feel.

Alice, I can't say for sure why we crashed. It could have been from being overloaded, or could have been a mechanical failure. We will never know for sure. The decision to go was with both John and I. I have an instrument ticket and that was why I was listed as the aircraft commander. John was in charge of the mission. At any time one of us could have said," this is too much." We could have quit the mission and others would have respected the wishes of the other pilot. I wish now that I had done just that. It was a dangerous mission and maybe we should have turned it down. I don't know for sure. If foresight was as good as hindsight we would never get into trouble. Also your John was a good pilot and a complete man. We both were out of the aircraft on each trip into the Landing Zone checking what was to out on the next trip.

We both took the word of the LoadMaster as to how many sheets of tin he had in each stack. We both made it out twice before with similar loads. So I don't know what happened except we lost power over 100 feet trees and no place to go. Believe me Alice, I thought I was trapped. I couldn't move and said to myself, "God, I'm trapped and will burn to death." Some thing said struggle and try to get out. I felt with my hand and found my armor release, I couldn't see because my helmet was down over my face. I released the armor and then the seat belt. I could only move downward with difficulty. I came out a hole in the Plexiglass nose and saw we were on fire. I yelled back in the hole, "John get out we are on fire."

I tired to get back in but the smoke was too thick. The hole I came out of was too small to get back in. His seat was broken off and fell down over mine. I was in the right seat and the ship hit the ground on the right side. If his seat hadn't come loose he would have been okay. He said his legs were caught. I tried to tear a bigger hole in the plexiglass with my hands so I could get in to turn his seat around and release him. He was facing the rear of the aircraft head down and all I could see was the back of the seat. I tore plastic till I was pulled away from the ship. I'm sure the smoke got to John long before I quit tearing at the plexiglass. Alice I hope you know that I did all that I could to get John. Yes, there was a bond between us now made by John. I would like to see you on my return to the states. I have your address now and will certainly try to see you if I come into Travis. I wish that I could have seen you in Bangkok. I was there in July on R&R. I will be returning to the states on 15 February 67 I hope. I intend to retire the end of February. I will have twenty in the army in February. I will be thirty eight this month so I don't think it will be hard to find a job on the outside.

I transferred to the 147th here at Vung Tau on 5 October. When Major Shields left the 178th I wanted to leave also and volunteered to come to the 147th. I have been doing quite a bit of flying down here. I have been back to Dau Tieng many times since the accident. There is a major battle going on in that area right now. I stood on the Dau Tieng airstrip a few days ago and watched a Huey crash into the village. It had the 1st Division aviation brigade commander on it. I don't think anyone got out of that crash. We have been lucky with the Chinook lately. I hope it stays that way.

Alice, I hope I haven't opened old wounds. I sure don't want to upset you. Please accept my apology for not writing sooner. Give the boys a hug and kiss for me. You can tell them that their dad was all man.

I'll close for now. Drop me a line or two if you get the chance. I'll try not to be so long in answering any more letters.

Sincerely,

Josh

Chapter 8- "I'm Giving You My Wings"

I came of age-into a consciousness of the wider world, I should say, during two epochal events in American history…the withdrawal from Vietnam in 1972 and then Watergate. It seems now the greatest harm we did was to our own psyche. We attached ourselves to the notion that as a nation we were victims of the Vietnam War and Watergate.

The lowered bar of expectation morphed into a "we can't" attitude. Our robust and vital nation always seeking more; always expanding; always optimistic began to husband its energies; prune its dreams.

Now, well into a new century we are chafed by an obsession with limitations: limitations of the environment as well as limited in the notion of what is possible. Instead the communal labels that began with defeat in Vietnam and betrayal by Watergate have infected our individual DNA's.

Now, we are victims on an individual scale…a child cannot be expected to achieve for because its ADHD; a Mother cannot be a good parent because they were, themselves, verbally abused as a child; an inner city kid has no voices saying 'You Can.' because these children are constantly reminded they are 'economically deprived'; 'socially challenged'; or whatever label is the latest to allow our youth the incorporate a victim label to themselves. It seems we take the wind out of their sails before they have a chance to put their boat in the water.

1966 was a good year to die for my father. He did not have to see the culture war explode; see his wife marginalized if she stayed at home raising John's boys instead of burning her bra. "Big John" didn't have to see his fellow pilots go back-and back-and back as one "hooch-buddy" did for four tours in Vietnam. Each tour interrupted by time back in the States to watch the campus unrest; our inner cities explode in rage; and the First Amendment used to protect the rights of a person to wear a shirt that said "Fuck the Draft."

In 1999 I received my father's personnel records from St. Louis. In a sea of bureaucratic indifference, one good man mailed me Dad's personnel file from the National Personnel Records Center there in St. Louis with a letter that said "Perhaps, this may help your search to learn more…"

Layer-by-excruciating-layer the facts of the crash tore at every vessel of my heart of how Dad was incinerated for his country on June 27, 1966.

Yet, the safety net breaking the fall was a stream of e-mails from those who knew Dad or, if these Vietnam veterans did not know him, they would extend condolences. Every helicopter unit in Vietnam was listed at vhfcn.org in numerical order. In each Guestbook my entry read: "my father-Cpt. John S. Seeley was KIA on 6-27-66 when his CH-47 crashed in the 'Iron Triangle. If you knew or served with 'Big John' e-mail me at markseeley@........"

One pilot who responded served with my father in Korea. He shared a very funny memory that was especially poignant given the fact he was the only one to survive. Ben Humphreys was killed in the crash Dad described in his letter in chapter one in Korea, Pete Gorvad and my father in Vietnam. Here is that memory:

John, Pete Gorvad and I lived in the small hooch at Camp K-6 down near the tennis court. We had additional duties. Captain Gorvad, Infantry Airborne Special Forces was the adjutant. John was the billeting officer, I was the officer for the club, and CWO2 Ben Humphreys was the Special Services officer.

One night after dinner in the Open Mess John, Pete, and I hatched a plan to have some fun with Ben Humphreys. We decided to have Pete ask Ben to requisition a "Tennis Ball Refuzzing Machine" for Ben to submit to the Korean Special Services in Seoul. We all agreed if Ben came to us to verify the existence of these refuzzing machines we would implore him to get one. This was because we couldn't get enough tennis balls due to the fact that the tennis court was poured concrete and just tore the covers off the balls. He was convinced we were conning him, but we prevailed and he finally asked for the "refuzzer." Your dad kept asking him when the "refuzzer" was due and Ben didn't catch on until he received a due out. Pete had called a friend in Seoul and told him what we were doing and we needed an official looking due out for a "refuzzer." Ben was a good sport about it and we all had fun teasing him about his supply know how!

Father went through flight school in 1959; then served with his first H-21 transport helicopter company at Fort Ord from '60-'61. I was born 12-26-60. Then he went to Korea-deployed ultimately for 15 months. This overseas tour extended 3 months involuntarily by our forces going on full alert. What had happened? The East Germans were building the Berlin Wall. Then, father had to go through a National Security Clearance to fly for the 3rd Helicopter Company out of Ft. Belvoir.

Of course, I do not know why he was chosen for this duty, but it seemed logical given the fact he had hauled VIP's around in Korea as you know from reading his Korea letters in Chapter 1.

Recently, the HISTORY CHANNEL did a documentary on an underground bunker the government completed in 1961. Situated in the West Virginia country-side attached to the Grienbrier Golf Resort, this bunker had 6-inch steel doors and enough space for the First Family, Cabinet, Supreme Court Justices and all 535 elected members of

Congress. Had the nuclear missiles flown the pilots of my father's unit would have flown the muckety-mucks to this shelter. Mom commented to me once about those years 1962-1964 and the Cuban Missile Crisis in particular by saying: "Heck, Mark I did not see John for days…he was restricted to barracks as they waited for the red phone to ring."

Well, this posting allowed my father to see a piece of history on one of our nation's saddest days. He wrote of the day's events to Grandad who lived in California after he got home that night. So, Grandad had been half- right…two men of great historical note had walked by my father the day of JFK's assassination, but not at Andrews AFB. My grandfather passed in 1984. My father's sister-my aunt Cynthia turned this letter and two others over to me about five years ago. My uncle Bill and her were preparing to retire and move from the Central California home they had lived in for 45 years as public school teachers. They were going through 45 years of stuff they had accumulated. Found among things she had saved from Grandad when he died was the confirmation my un-diagnosed manic-depressive Grandfather had it half-right as to what his son saw on Nov. 22 '63.

22 Nov 63

Dear Dad-
This is certainly a day that all of us will not forget soon. I thought that I should write to you a few lines-stating the events as I have witnessed them here today.
I had a rough instrument flight today that lasted through the lunch hour and went home for a late lunch. I arrived back at the field at 1:50 and as I walked through the hangar to the standby room I heard the PA set over the sound of rivet and air-guns but paid no attention to the cold and unusual voice. Upon entering the Pilots Standby Room I was followed by a crew-chief who announced it to the coffee crowd. Everyone refused to believe it and there were momentary obscene shouts of disbelief. I remember saying "Shut the hell up and lets see what the TV

*says'- and walked over to the set and turned it on. At that time the news
was that he had been wounded and was in the Hospital. About an hour
later the news came through that the President was dead.*

*Training aircraft in the Pattern were asked to land and a few
minutes later I was alerted to proceed to Fort McNair in a VIP H-21
along with another aircraft-to standby for orders from the Commanding
General-Military District of Washington. We left as soon as possible
along the emergency flight route over the Potomac and landed at
McNair-across from Haines Point. We were there about an hour and one
half when further orders came through for me to takeoff and report to the
Pentagon Heliport and standby to transport the Chief of Staff-Army to
Andrews AFB. We arrived there-a ten minute flight, at dusk and the
Helipod and grass area adjacent was already occupied by three Air
Force H-21's-soon afterward another H-21 came in from Belvoir to back
me up. We continued to wait for our passengers but in a national
emergency such as this Gen. Wheeler was tied to his command post and
did not depart the Pentagon for Andrews to meet AF#1 upon its landing.
I went inside the Control Tower to be available at the telephone and also
to monitor the radio frequencies-which were busy with military air
traffic-many choppers coming into and going out of the D.C. area to
Andrews and other points-picking up VIP's*

*At 5:30 PM a black sedan arrived-it was dark now and
McNamara, Gen. Taylor and Bobby Kennedy stepped out in that order to
board the AF chopper for Andrews. Needless to say, they were a grim lot
as they walked by me. The Attorney General was stooped and seemed in
a daze. McNamara walked straight and I noticed his fists were clenched.*

*At 6:15 we were notified to return to Belvoir. The Pentagon was
lit up full blast and the parking lost was still full. The traffic out of D.C.
was late tonight and jammed bumper-bumper. On take off I looked
behind and noticed the downtown district of Washington was dim from
businesses closing down-theatres and so on.*

*I spent the entire flight of twenty minutes either trying to
establish the proper radio calls and for relaying messages from other
choppers. AF#1 was landing about now and the radio traffic was fierce.*

*Back at Belvoir-the C.O. met me and wanted to know what I had
been involved in since there were so damned many aircraft involved. I
told him that nothing important and reported to Operations to close out
my Flt. plan and go home if allowed.*

*I walked into the house and Doug told me that our President was
dead and that it was a sad day. So I picked him up after awhile and told
him all about it and that a little boy didn't have a daddy anymore.*

And thats about it from here-the kids are asleep now and Alice is laying down with a headache.

I still can't believe it and am slightly outraged by the whole affair. I thought I'd send these few lines about the little bit of History I saw today here in D.C.

Love
John

In early 1964, my father accepted a direct commission to 1st Lieutenant. Shortly thereafter our vagabond Army life led to his posting at Ft. Wainwright, Alaska with the 65th Helicopter Company.

It's here where stale, emotionless photographic memories of him began. As we drove to Alaska Dad allowed me to sit on his lap and 'steer' the VW family van. At some point we had to put the car on a ferry and I remember us driving into the 'garage' of the ship. I remember driving my little T-Bird pedal car…recall sitting in an unusually high chair in the Anchorage Alaska hospital. Some kidney problem gave me a temperature of 106 degrees for days. Mom gave me cold baths to no avail. Finally, she told me she took me in tears to the base hospital. I was taken by helicopter to Anchorage.

After my release someone snapped a photo of the four of us standing in front of the hospital. Clearly visible were cracks in the 7-story hospital for the Great Earthquake had happened just months before.

In 2004 I located a retired Colonel who was my father's Operations Officer at Ft. Wainwright. He remembered my father fondly and shared this in an e-mail:

As Operations Officer, I assigned pilots to the daily flights and quickly learned that John was a "perfectionist pilot" who could be relied upon to be prepared for any mission no matter how demanding.

During the spring thaw of 1964 we received a call that a small Native Alaskan village was being flooded and had requested evacuation to a safer location. Without hesitation I called on John to take a flight of two ships and move people to higher ground while the rest of the unit loaded food and tents to support a temporary refuge.

When John reached the village it was already under water in most locations. He found a sandbar in the river that would support the helicopters during the evacuation and the crews of both ships immediately began to escort the residents to safety. With the water rising rapidly, John and his colleagues were able to evacuate all residents-and yes, their sled dogs-to a safe location. Before nightfall, a new camp was erected where the evacuees would remain in relative comfort until the flood waters receded.

On this and many other occasions, John Seeley's commitment to professionalism stood as a beacon for all those who served with him. I was proud to have known him

Was it any wonder my father rose from Private-to-Captain? In the pine box I found a three page proposal I'm certain Dad pounded out on a home typewriter. It was stamped "approved", "approved" at its end. Dad proposed the pilots carry Polaroid cameras in the H-21 cockpits and when they found a good landing zone on that frozen Alaska tundra they should snap a photo of it and share it with other pilots. In his personnel records officer evaluation forms mention was made of him rescuing two fishermen whose boat was overturned in the Tanana River.

Yet, his most noted act had happened years earlier. A thank you letter from the Barstow County Sheriff's and a newspaper article were preserved in the pine box as well. Dad was on TDY at Fort Irwin. A baby had wandered into the desert from a home bordering it. A search ensued. For over three hours no one could find the baby…night had fallen and temps. had dropped…then Warrant Officer Seeley spotted a dropped diaper and flew out in concentric circles until his helicopter had the bare-bottomed baby in the grace of the chopper's searchlight.

At one point in 1998-99 I was receiving an average of an e-mail a week with the subject heading: "I knew your dad." Each one I received treated the bleeding wound of my father's horrific death-by-fire.

The chance to do more than just read of John Seeley's career was possible because his Vietnam unit, the 178th "Boxcars", held annual reunions. I attended three of these in the years 1998, 2000, and 2003. At each reunion the surviving pilot was there. Though questions had arisen regarding his conduct the day of the crash, we never discussed this at these reunions. Their purpose was to rekindle the camaraderie of that long ago time: not revisit the bad or the painful.

Each reunion brought a special moment or memory I hold close to now. At the first reunion I arrived to find a Major my father wrote of slugging in a fight in his final letter had checked with the desk clerk numerous times as to whether I had arrived. The VA had done a search of VA records from TDY orders I'd found in Dad's records. I had 'Hooked' him up to the Association by writing him with the information about that 1998 reunion.

Like my father, this Major was very tall. At one point during the reunion he asked me to accompany him to the airport because he needed to double-check something on his return ticket from the reunion. After he came out of the terminal and got back in the car, I asked "Big Eddie" about the fight Dad mentioned. He said he was certain it never happened with the remark "'Big John" and me get into a fight-no way!"

Walking into the Hospitality Room of the 2000 reunion for the first time I was nervous. Immediately, I looked for the surviving pilot. Through these three reunions I was never able to shake the awkwardness; the thought I was in the company of men much greater than myself. So, the friendly, gregarious personality of John Logan became a magnet I was drawn to. I usually hovered close to him.

When I walked up to him at the 2000 reunion in that Hospitality Room he was talking to another 178th veteran. The man asked who I was.

Josh replied: "This is John Seeley's son, Mark."

This other pilot smiled ear-to-ear and said: "John Seeley's son! I served with John Seeley-3rd 'Herd' at Fort Belvoir." He gave me a vigorous handshake. I learned this pilot had arrived in-country with the 178th "Boxcars" in the fall of 1966. His tour was shortened when, on final approach into Phu Loi, a lucky VC shot up through the bubble canopy, shredded his leg and he earned his Purple Heart and a trip home to recover from his wounds.

At the 2003 reunion I went to lunch with a pilot who had watched our family say what would be our final goodbye at the Port of Oakland and a second member of the Accident Board that examined Dad's crash. Both had left their Vietnam units to fly for Air America. Very telling was the fact the Accident Board member said he had never felt comfortable with the surviving pilot's witness statement to the Accident Board and had no desire to meet the surviving pilot who was next door at the 178th Reunion hotel. So modest are these men about their accomplishments it was years later I learned the Accident Board member was the pilot of the helicopter in that iconic photo of the last helicopter to take off from atop the Saigon embassy when Saigon fell to the Communists in 1975.

The following e-mail is a vivid reminder this group of men smiling and back-slapping each other were not old fraternity brothers, but soldiers whose laughter and smiles masked much different memories. As one crew chief with the 178th who arrived in-country just a few months after my father's death related in an e-mail the after effects of combat make them more than just memories. He wrote:

> I started having war-related nightmares, intrusive thoughts, and flashbacks when I was at Ft. Stewart in 1968 and didn't even know what a flashback was. I relived one firefight a hundred times and I dream in full color and sound, even smells. Did you know that the combined sounds of six rotor blades and two M-60 machine guns make a syncopated percussive rhythm that is more intense than any rock band could make? Talk about the music in my head... I rarely have flashbacks or war dreams anymore; when I do I record them in a journal. Even today, I can shut my eyes and see through gunsights, and when I fly a light plane I still tend to scan tree lines looking for muzzle flashes or tracers...hardly ever receive any ground fire here in Minnesota! Anyway, I was just an enlisted crewman who was in combat for seven months; the VHPA guys are pilots, many of whom did several tours in Vietnam.

In 1999 I located an enlisted man named Marvin Graese. Again, it was research from those TDY orders I'd found in the pine box.

Marvin didn't know his unit from his Vietnam service of 33 years earlier had an Association. He begged his doctor to allow him to attend the 1999 Philadelphia reunion of the 178th Boxcars. His doctor said no. Two months before I attended the 2000 reunion I called Marvin to ask him if he was going to the 2000 reunion hosted by a 1966 crew chief. No, there was no hope of him making it. The man was only sixty two years old, but he was dying of kidney cancer. He was convinced it was from a second tour in Vietnam in a ground unit that was showered regularly with Agent Orange. I promised Marvin I would stand up at the 178th Banquet held on the final day and ask the guys to keep Marvin in their thoughts and/or prayers.

The day I returned from the 2000 reunion I asked Mom to stop by my P.O. Box before dropping me off at my place. Marvin had told how proud he was of "his boy" who was serving in the United States Army as a Commissioned Officer. The letter informed me his father had died one month after my last conversation with his dad. He wrote: "Words cannot express what it meant to my father to have phone reunions with his Vietnam buddies in the last year-and-a-half of his life."

At these reunions I would fight my manic-depressive urge to talk, talk, talk I did manage to do some listening and heard some humbling stories of the devotion and service these men Gave...these Vietnam veterans spurned by many of their fellow citizens when they came home and vilified by the media after Vietnam was lost.

One pilot mentioned how he had been in the Korean War as an infantryman. He survived the Hell that ensued when the Chinese crossed the Yalu River. Yes, this pilot was one of the "Chosin Few."

One crew member had been at the 1998 "Mother Rucker" reunion. He was a bust-up...a very funny man. Yet, I was told his humor hid great pain he felt from being a crew member on the first Boxcar that crashed on May 30, 1966.Two Majors fell short of a mountainside re-supply LZ on the side of Nui Ba Den Mountain. Dad wrote of this crash that had happened while Dad was in the Camp Drake hospital in Japan. The crew chief Ross Brown and one member of the 1st Infantry Division were killed.

At the 2000 reunion he asked me one morning to go outside with him to the pool-side area accessible by a sliding glass door. He passed me a short story he had written about the crash. It was all too graphic for he mentioned the fire that consumed the craft. I thought to myself as I read it: "He must know my father burned-to-death." Yet, I read it and gave him some writing advice.

At that 2000 reunion the surviving pilot and two others from years '66-'67 who knew Dad stood evaluating me. One commented that my father would have never had the pot-belly I do, but that with my blonde hair and blue eyes I had the coloring my Dad did. Then they said: "Yeah, we always said your Dad looked like a poor man's Lee Marvin"

Three years later I was found by one of my father's cousins after I remembered my father on a Memorial Day weekend national radio show. The host, Rusty Humphries, is a radio talk-show host. On the weekends he is part of 'Talk Radio Network America' and his show is broadcast nationwide. Mr. Humphries father was killed in Vietnam when he was a boy. One Saturday I got off work and turned on my car radio to hear him say: "We are not talking Bush…or Clinton…today's broadcast is on Memorial Day weekend. If you knew someone-family or friend-who gave their lives in service to our country call in…"

So happens John Seeley's cousin's husband was driving home in Reno. He got home and told his wife: "I think your cousin just got remembered on a national radio broadcast."

Two days later I got an e-mail with a family photo of Dad's side of the family taken in 1950 I had never seen. John Seeley's cousin had called her son in St. Louis and asked her own son to use his computer skills to find me.

Of course, phone contact and an actual meeting took place in Boise within a few months since her own daughter lived here. Yet, in one of our phone conversations she said: "Mark, I am mailing you a BIOGRAPHY Channel documentary about the life of Lee Marvin.

Johnny not only looked kind of like Lee Marvin, but Johnny's mannerisms were a lot like Lee Marvin's."

Of course, Vietnam is a passionate issue. Thus, the wider community of those directly affected by it: the veterans, their families, and the families of those on the Vietnam Wall do not always agree. The controversy over the design of the Vietnam Wall itself underscores this point.

Whether right or wrong, I have had my own differences with others whose fate was somehow tethered to the Vietnam War.

One month after "Angel, I Write These Things…" by John S. Seeley as told by his son Mark was published in the BOISE WEEKLY for Memorial Day weekend 1997, the Moving Wall came to Boise for its now-defunct river festival. The Marine Corps League was manning the computers and guiding people to the Names on the Wall. I found a veteran who looked to be of the age of someone who may have been in Vietnam. He was wearing a red beret and guiding people to the Names.

"Are you a Vietnam veteran sir?" I asked.

"Marine Infantry in Vietnam!" he said with conviction.

I unfolded an actual issue where "Angel, I Write These Things…" was its cover/feature story. As I unfolded it to show it to him, I said: "I just wanted to share my father's story with you…"

He cut me off and bellowed back at me with such force in his voice that I took two steps back. He pointed at the article and said: "I read that a month ago. You need to reprint that and pass it out to visitors here at the Moving Wall!"

Since he had been in Vietnam in the worst of the muck, mire, and combat I heeded his advice and met with a BOISE WEEKLY staffer on how to make reprints. I passed out 250 with this message in the margin: "This is one of 58, 209 (the current final total as of 1997) stories of honor. They did not choose to die so it also reflects the service of those who went to Vietnam and returned home alive as well. It's in this spirit I share my father's story."

Sadly, I guess inter-service rivalry reared its sometimes ugly head. Most of the Marine veterans would not read it and treated me as if I was deranged and obsessed because I was there at the Moving Wall each day. Yet I was there passing out reprints at the suggestion of one of their men.

I resigned from the 178th Boxcar Association after my attempt to stand in at an official photograph taken at the Pensacola 2003 reunion led to a debacle when one of the 178th wives shouted at me to "get out of the picture because you are not military."

I had simply wanted to hold a 178th hat in missing-man style for my Dad. After that photograph the 178th Assoc. visited a half-size replica of the Vietnam Wall there in Pensacola. A 178th pilot who arrived in-country in October 1966 was the host of that reunion. Lucky for me, I was his passenger as we drove over from the Naval Air Museum to the replica of the Wall. He persuaded me to hold my fire because I was ready to say to the 178th wife once we began to walk down into the Names, "My father's name is here. Stop and don't walk down into the Names because you're a wife-you are not military."

I have been to the actual Wall in Washington D.C. twice. The first visit was for the reunion of a group I joined in 2003 formally by paying the dues. Modeled after the WWII Orphans Network, it was founded by the son of a downed Air Force pilot. The group, Sons And

Daughters In Touch (sdit.org), is open to veterans as well, but our common bond is our fathers are on the Vietnam Veterans Memorial in Washington D.C. It is estimated there are 20,000 grown children of those on the Wall. SDIT membership numbers in the thousands. SDIT reunions at the Wall are held every five years.

My mother and I flew back to Washington D.C. My brother Doug flew up from Florida and we were all together for SDIT Father's Day weekend at the Wall in 2005. My mother had visited in 1987 with my step-father, but it was the first visit for my brother and I. In the years since the 1997 Moving Wall, I had been to other visits the Moving Wall made to Idaho.

My mother, brother, and I went down to the actual Wall in D.C. the night of our arrival. I thought I would cry: I certainly had at the Moving Wall. Yet, the Wall was so beautiful at night I just stood there in silent reverence feeling the enormity of the treasure we lost in that war... 58,248 men and eight female nurses.

My second visit to the Wall was on Veterans Day 2007 for the 25th Anniversary of its construction. For only the fourth time since it was built all 58,256 (four names were added Memorial Day 2008) names were read by volunteers...30 names at a time. It took three-and-a-half days. The readings started at 4 p.m. on November 7 until midnight. Then the readings were from 5 a.m. to midnight for three days!

Requests to read a name had to be submitted to the Vietnam Veterans Memorial Fund by late August. I received my list of 30 names to read in September. I researched all the names and learned 9 of the 30 died in helicopter-related crashes. Above my father on Line 101 on Panel 8E was a pilot named Jerry McNabb. I found his widow and called her to tell her I would be reading his name.

She said: "I never re-married and raised our three children myself. I knew I would never find someone as special as my Jerry."

Her husband's name was one of the first I read. Seconds later I read John S. Seeley at 9:58 p.m. on Wednesday November 7.

Through the wonders of the modern Internet Mrs. McNabb mailed an 8 1/2 by 11 paper with a photo of "her Jerry" and my wife encased it in plastic and laid it under the Panel 8E for Mrs. McNabb while I left copies of two letters of John Seeley's I had published in the BOISE WEEKLY in 2006 and 2007.

On this visit to the Wall, I paid special attention to visiting other names on this Wall of Honor of men father had served with who also Gave All in Vietnam...a LTC Colonel named Pete Gorvad who was Infantry and was born the same exact day as Dad: April 10 1932. They had served at Camp K-6 in Korea in 1961. His unit was under attack on March 8, 1969. As he met with his staff a mortar-round landed square on his command tent and killed him and eight of his men. Over the years of research I had tried to learn more about Frank Roop (1959 flight classmate) and the following pilots of the 6th Tran. (Korea ['61-'62] who appear in a company photograph with Dad): Alton Gajan, William "Handsome" House, John Eddy, George Clarke, and Boyd Morrow.

Other than their Vietnam Wall data, the search was futile with two exceptions. One pilot I located did not know my father, but was a CH-54 'Skycrane' pilot. Not only did he recover Frank Roop's crashed CH-47, but he knew Alton Gajan who was killed in the first CH-54 accident with fatalities. He remembers Alton Gajan's "can-do" attitude.

Gajan's trademark statement was: "If it rotates and creates lift, I can fly it!"

The second veteran was a pilot who shared the same quarters with my father and Pete Gorvad in Korea. He had been a close friend of Boyd Morrow. Boyd Morrow was the Maintenance Officer for a Huey Unit in Vietnam. He was flight-testing a repaired Huey in 1967 when he lost his "Jesus nut" and flipped over in a rice paddy. Incredibly, he survived with a broken arm. He laid in a field hospital as the nurses dealt with more serious cases...a blood clot hit his brain and killed him...leaving his wife a widow and his three children fatherless.

One cannot hear such stories without coming to know of the value of each Name on the Wall. This is what led to me resigning from SDIT. A number of SDIT members made the trek to Washington D.C. to read their father's name in November 2007. Most brought a remembrance to put at the Panel where their father's name is inscribed.

One of our members leaned a huge portrait of photos of her Dad against the Wall. Seeing this portrait completely block out at least ten lines of Names, I protested to this SDIT member.

I was alarmed by her response: "If the National Park Service has a problem with it, then they can talk to me."

I had a huge problem with it. I told an NPS Ranger and he determined she should find a stand to place the portrait on.

I said to the founder of SDIT: "We will find out if this organization is about them...the Names on the Wall or about staying silent and placating the egos of our own members." Sadly, the latter was true. I have been open about my mental illness for years now. So, my passion for protecting the integrity of the Names was treated by some SDIT members as the ranting of a mentally ill person.

Yet, I did not allow this sad turn of events to mar the experience of being there for the Reading of the Names. For three and a half days the names were read 30 at a time. The three full days began at 5 a.m. and ended at midnight. There were not enough volunteers for every set of 30 names so many of us volunteered for what was termed as "gap reading." One of the nights I was standing in line to "gap read" when the lady next to me said she was a Gold Star mother. Her son, CW3 H. Dan McCants Jr. had been a Blackhawk pilot, but upon learning the 160th Special Operations Aviation Regiment was short of CH-47 pilots her son had transitioned into the CH-47. He was killed in a CH-47 crash in Afghanistan on February 18, 2007: a sobering reminder that as we honored these Vietnam fallen, sacrifices were being made again by our finest now in another controversial war.

My grandfather had raised Dad to respect politicians so one chance meeting meant a lot to me. I had just bought coffee across the street from the Wall one of those mornings. As I crossed the street, I noticed Senator Ted Kennedy and an entourage getting into the back of a limousine. I walked up and extended my hand and passed the Senator a copy of "Angel, I Write These Things..." by John S. Seeley as told by his son Mark. I did not tell him mother said they both voted for Nixon in '60, but briefly described Dad's letter the day his older brother John was assassinated and that Robert had walked by my father at the Pentagon heli-port. I'm certain he must have just completed a 'gap reading' just as two Congressmen I'd already met-Congressman Shays and Pearlmutter-had done.

On our last morning in Washington D.C. my wife and I had breakfast with the veteran who had been my father's Operations Officer at Fort Wainwright '64-'65. We met at the hotel's restaurant. I sat directly across from him with my wife at my side.

At the close of the meeting he said: "Mark, I'm giving you my Wings. When you found me you asked for good memories of your father, but that led me to remember some things I needed to process and bring some peace to."

He then said: "Let me cite two. I commanded a small Huey unit in 1967. One day before I was scheduled to go home I was alerted that my tent mate had gone down and that we had to recover his body. I flew to the crash area, met with a ground unit, and brought him out of the jungle. I flew back to the base but he was evacuated in a ground vehicle. Carrying him out in a body bag was one of the worst things I ever had to do. A second memory was when our base was overrun while I was in Hawaii on leave. The VC had taken one of our supply troops. We searched and searched, but found where they held him in the jungle too late. We discovered he had left a popcorn trail by tearing off bits of his military I.D. card so, if we found their hiding spot in time, we would know in which direction they were moving. It was years later that I read his name on a casualty list. I had hoped he would return with the POW's but he never showed."

The veteran then said: "I'm sorry Mrs. Seeley. I didn't mean to upset you." I'd been so intent on his words, I had not noticed tears streaming down my wife's cheeks. As I looked to my left to see this, my wife said: "No, sir. It's okay. It's just that I try to tell my husband the good he is doing for Vietnam veterans, but this is too much."

These Wings were no larger than an inch between thumb and forefinger. A perfect fit for the space on a hat I proudly wore. Between a knitted reproduction of a CH-47 and the words "CH-47 Chinook" spelled out in a semi-oval above it was the perfect spot for these Wings.

That afternoon I was back down at the Wall wanting to spend as much time as I could that final day "with Dad." As I stood in front of Panel 8E a man commented; "Wow, your father was a Colonel!"

I replied contemptuously: "My father wasn't a Colonel. He was a Captain."

The man pointed at the wings on the hat. I said: "Oh that. Its aviator's Wings from a man who was a Major when Dad was in Alaska..."

He cut me off my explanation and said: "No, they're not...that's a Colonel's Eagle."

Here at this place that remembers those who Gave All, I was once again reminded of how so little is known by John Q. Public of the import of the first half of that phrase...All Gave Some. What our Vietnam veterans Gave-and the pain they carry-is something they rarely share and they speak of their own achievements even less.

Chapter 9-"...Once Again Believe in a Loving God"

There's a famous saying that there are "no atheists in foxholes." Well, I've never been in a foxhole or near one so I cannot speak to the veracity of that statement.

As you know from my trek through that homeless winter, I had-and have-no God.

One of my father's most profound letters was one of the ones his sister found packing to move from her working home of over 45 years. He wrote it from the hospital in Saigon just before being shipped out to Japan. He was smack dab-in-the-middle of the comedy of medical maladies and errors that plagued him in his 90 days in-country before he went in body bag.

> *May 16, 1966*
> *Saigon*

My Dearest Sister:

I am writing to you now because efforts to find a birthday card of late have proved fruitless. I do not want another end of May to pass by without sending you my devotion and love.

I am writing this from a hospital in Saigon. Nothing serious-my legs just gave out and I was exhausted and so I was admitted here for a complete examination. All test thus far have been negative and so now I am the property of the "Bug Doctor", what a thing to have on my records!

I feel guilty for even being in here-with so many men about me with honest and terribly real reasons for being here. Lying here, looking at the ceiling, I have time to search out many memories and dwell upon them with both fondness-and remorse. I am not in remorse for the life I have lived to date and have the blessed nod of good fortune in having acquired a good woman, better than I deserve-and from our union, two young sons that are the hopes and dreams of my existence. I think about them often- and the memory of their seeking eyes and the feel of their arms about me is the yeast that sustains my will to survive this sad and brutal war.

I will not expound upon my own individual exploits or acts while under fire because they are, at best, shallow, if not transparent when held against those deeds of these shattered men lying alongside of me. Further, I do not wish my Alice to know of things as they really are with me over here. My letters to her consist in the most part, of discussions of household matters and while they deter her knowledge of my own collision with reality, they are also a tonic to me.

Yet in my observations and discussions here I have discovered a profound truth- and I would be remiss if I did not share this with you. This concerns our precious David and his boyhood. If I trespass into the sacred world of your own parental decisions, then please forgive me-but some of my blood runs in David's being and with or without qualifications-I feel I own some claim to this wonderful boy.

I recall mentioning to you that I allowed to some extent, perhaps to excess, the use of war-like toys for my children-explaining it away as saturation, hoping that it was a phase that would eventually pass away. Millions are being made each year over the sale of such toys, something that you and I cannot prevent during our own children's formative years. Years from now-beyond our horizon, perhaps, the world will have had its fill of torn flesh. But for now, we are bombarded with its manifestations of misery and it contaminates those innocent years of our children.

As a pilot, my sojourns aloft are still rewarding as I seek the cleansing world of elements somewhat in concert with my own chemistry. Yet my tasks over here often require the witnessing of men mangled beyond my will to describe-and the return to earth and its harsh realities has caused me to ponder if there is any sanctuary in this world-void of the hue of red.

These men-boys really, that occupy beds next to my own are all World War II babies and they grew up with mama it seems, so busy were their fathers trying to salvage a life and years robbed them during the war. Also, during their boyhood years, their fathers had their fill of war and toys of violence were not in style. Now, suddenly, they have been thrust into a war without redemption-a conflict that will continue somewhere on the globe for years to come. I discover that the great majority of these men did not play with those toys you find objectionable and so now they 'play' with the real things. All too often, they die without purpose in their own minds. Those who live reveal this. They sacrifice-not for an obscure cause-but for each other. This seems their first chance at the 'game'-and before they can adjust and place values in their proper prospective, they pay a price for participation.

These observations, Cynthia-are my own observations. I could be totally in error, yet I suspect not.

As for myself-by comparison, I had those toys and grew up playing at war-emulating the Saturday movie heroes-and in the process, placed honor and duty somewhere below my first instinct-to survive in any situation. If these are the words of a person somewhat less than a man-then so be it. Color me yellow. My standards of conduct are not in question by my associates and comrades-so alike are our ages and flesh and blood commitments across the ocean. I hope all of the above serves as an introduction to what-if I may be allowed, to suggest to you in regards [to] David.

Sis-let him play 'Bang-bang-your-dead.' Let him fall to the ground clutching his chest or head. Let him hide behind trees and bushes-and win or lose, do battle against good and evil. Let his own mind seek out those values denied these kids over here. From time to time, he will tire of it, but lessons will be learned, I am sure.

The love and warmth of his home will replace the winning and losing of the conflict of the day. Remember the lullaby that mother used to sing to me? "little man you're crying-you've had a busy day Jimmy stole your kiddie-car away...The enemy is out of sight. Sunday school will teach him that there is a God-and good and evil. My own heart bursts with joy at what my boys discover each Sunday. Perhaps thru them, I can once again believe in a loving God. But for now, I have yet to discover Him in the album of my years. I do subscribe to Hell however-not in the hereafter, but right here on Earth.

This letter was meant to be a birthday greeting to a woman who is still in my memory- a little blue-eyed, blonde sister-an obligation for me to harbor and protect. As we grew, I failed in that endeavor and can never forgive myself. But if you will accept from me, now, these thoughts over my concern for David and his transition into our tortured world, perhaps I can redeem myself in your eyes.

Sis, look fondly at toys in the driveway and dirty elbows-and books and blocks scattered at random. To me, now, the sight of these things is priceless and are all too soon put away in the closet of our memories. Enjoy each other, each day then, and God Bless and protect all of you.

With Love,
John

Mom did find us a church after Dad shipped over to Vietnam. I can see clearly-in my mind's eye-sitting in the little chair learning about the Lamb and Jesus. I don't know, but there was a certain kind of violence in how abruptly we were torn away from God. From Sunday School every Sunday to no God in the house after my father's death.

Thus, I've never been able to break through to a faith-to a belief in God. Most assuredly, there have been Christians who've driven me further from it. When I've mentioned my mother pulling us out of church, I've had her judged as wrong. I then ask them if they lost both parents and a spouse before the age of 30...none who have ever condemned my mother have said yes. They did not walk her walk...so they have no grounds on which to talk.

As deeply ensconced in my agnosticism as I am, I have still felt profoundly touched by Grace in this journey. Random atoms or mere chance seem a weak argument to some things that have happened in this decade-long trek to 'find' my Dad.

I spent three full days at the Moving Wall when it visited Boise in June of 1997 for the River Festival. As I shared earlier, I passed out 250 reprints of "Angel, I Write These Things..."

When the Moving Wall shut down I walked over the 'Friendship Bridge" to cross the river. I turned right to leave the paved Greenbelt and meet up with 13th St. for the short walk home. As I came over a very small hill there was a bicycle rental shop and parking lot with maybe 8 spaces to it. I noticed a pickup truck pull in that had Alaska plates, but a Department of Defense sticker. The driver and I crossed paths and I remarked: "I see your DOD sticker. We lived in Alaska when I was 4."

The driver said: "Yeah, I'm rarely there though. I travel the country under civilian contract investigating helicopter crashes. I'm here to investigate the one that killed the AF National Guard Major in Eastern Idaho. It's up in a box at Gowen Field"

I was astonished, but explained: "Sir, my father was killed in a CH-47 crash in Vietnam. He couldn't get out and they couldn't get in to free him."

"Well, the latest modification to the CH-47 is they can pull a string and the cockpit window falls out."

At the urging of a Marine who had been in Vietnam, I had just spent three days passing out reprints of "Angel..." at the Moving Wall as a healing measure. Could a cold, atheistic analysis explain what the statistical odds are of this chance meeting with this crash investigator?

Even more haunting is I knew the pilot of the crashed helicopter he was investigating. In that frozen Hell of homelessness in 1994-95, I had gone into a bar near my alma mater-BSU-for coffee a couple of times. One time I got in a conversation with the bartender. He was in the Army National Guard or Army Reserve and flew helicopters.

After talking about helicopters, the conversation shifted to how his biological father had been just a sperm donor. He explained his step-father had died recently, but this man was really his Dad. He was having a hard time coping with his loss.

I returned a few days later and gave the bartender/part-time helicopter pilot a letter. I wrote to him that whatever you believe doesn't have to make rational sense, but if you believe in it than it does not matter. I urged him to believe when the sun's warmth touched his skin to believe it was his step-father's-his true father's- love reaching him still.

As happened so often that winter I was thrown out of that bar without cause shortly after by the bar's owner. I only saw the helicopter pilot one more time. It was near the end of that homeless hell. I was walking back downtown from that Denny's near the airport that I would walk out to after the bar that served me coffee until 2 a.m. closed. It was a beautiful sunny day. A car stopped and someone yelled: "Would you like a ride?"

It was him. I told him: "No, I have bus fare, but it's such a beautiful day I've decided to walk." He thanked me for the note about the sun's warmth and said it had helped him so the least he could do was offer me a ride.

In November 1997 I had moved from the homeless shelter where I'd rented a third-floor apartment for two-and-a-half years. It was in an old colonial style house that had been divided into three apartments. Not long after moving I befriended my upstairs neighbor. Using their computer I began to put out Internet postings on military related websites "If you knew or served with John Seeley please e-mail me at: markseeley@........."

The very first veteran to reply was our neighbor at Fort Benning. Here is his e-mail:

Dear Mark,
In September, 1965 I moved into the Wedgefield Court apartment in Columbus, Georgia. On one side of me in the apartments was a Captain-Roger Donlon, a Medal of Honor winner from Vietnam. On the other side of our apartment was the Seeley family. Our family and the Seeley family became very good friends over the next 6 months. During that time, our two families went to a number of places together, the circus, the O Club among others.
I think I met your Dad the first day we moved into the apartment.

After just a few minutes, your Dad found out that I was an H-21 pilot. As a H-21 pilot himself, we develop a close relationship I have always treasured. I thought I'd end up in a Huey company, but John was determined I should be assigned to one of the Chinook companies the Army was also forming up at Fort Benning. John talked to the right people, and I was assigned to the not-yet-formed 179th. The 178th was already filled.

Anyone who has received a letter from your Dad, knows he was an extremely sensitive individual who could do a beautiful job of displaying that sensitivity in writing. I still have a letter your Dad wrote me from the ship taking him, and the rest of the 178th to Nam. I pull it out every Memorial Day and re-read it. I had been in Country a few weeks when I heard of the accident.

I replied with a long explanation in my e-mail of "Angel, I Write…" the Congressional Inquiry, and how this work into my father's life had evolved. In one sentence I wrote: "I have a few scarce memories-especially that final hug goodbye."

He e-mailed back: "Mark, perhaps your father can shed some light on his thoughts that day." Momentarily, I thought, "Cute, how is he going to that? He's dead." Tears streamed down my cheeks after I realized what I was reading.

I had wondered all my life what my father was thinking that day…in that moment of our final good-bye…in that suffocating embrace…and when I looked out the window to see tears creasing his face as he bade farewell to my brother and then my mother.

It is ironic the only peace I can find because I'm told closure will never come completely…the only peace is to believe that yes, there is a God, and that he chose my father to be the only pilot the 178th lost in 1966 in Vietnam…that God took him in such a horrible way, but told him that day-June 27, 1966-as he took my father's spirit home that one of his 'boys' would face severe trials and tribulations, but if his son passed these tests some healing could come for many scarred by our experience in Vietnam…and the foundation of this healing would be John Seeley's own letters.

Here is that letter to our Fort Benning neighbor. For me, it is the bridge that answered what my father thought the last time he held me in his arms. For the reader it is the first letter from John Seeley after he sailed away to war.

March 5, 1966

Dear Brian, Kris & Family-

Six days out at sea now on this old tub and all is well. The seas are more tranquil now that we are past Hawaii and entering the Tropics. Spent a long while on deck with book, suntan lotion, radio and deck chair- but no tour director to organize shuffleboard and etc. Bloody shame-that.

I wrote Alice and the boys for the first time since leaving the pier(the roll of the ship was excessive up till today and writing was near impossible)-and will post a few letters from Subic Bay in the Phillipine Islands. From there its a two day trip to Vung Tau and the 178th will have arrived before you receive this letter.

I think Alice wrote to you from our place in California after we got settled. Yet here's mine.

We made good time X-ing the states, arriving-or passing thru Stockton about the same time the lead choppers arrived there. Looked around for several days and moved into a very nice place north of Sacramento where I think they will be quite comfortable and content.

I consider myself a most fortunate man in that I was with my family all of the time until the ship pulled away from the pier. Then, I went through the roughest duty I've had in a long while. The boys were trying so hard to be brave but broke at the last as did I, and their arms around me as now will be vivid for an eternity. Alice put on her best face she could muster through her tears and I waved them goodbye until the car was out of sight and then went up on the deck to find a place amongst the aircraft where I let it all out.

San Francisco was never more beautiful than on that day and the night and the city even had the ship's crew pausing at the rail as we slipped into the bay. Then and only then, did all of this seem real and these last months all telescoped into one complete reality for me. In recalling this now I find myself warmed with the memories of our sojourn there at Benning. The children-the neighbors-the apartment.

I cannot recall any of this without harboring a very warm companionship towards your family and I feel that I should once again offer thanks to you folks for being the kind of people that you are.

Surely, Brian-you and I will meet on the other side and so I feel only a temporary loss of a friend. Yet our families-that seemed to congress so well may not have that opportunity again and I resent the circumstances that rob us as soon as we glean some valued friends in our pursuit of this kind of life. The boys genuinely miss their neighbors and Mark seems to have it in his mind that if Brian is going to follow me-then the famiily will follow to California. I wish it were so. It is for that feeling that I write to say my thanks-to all of you.

We still do not have an APO and so I am using the Port Authority APO at Vung Tau on the return address-just to get it in the mail-and that's about it from this end of the line.

I will be writing you Brian as we get set up over here- to the rest of you thanks again, God bless all of you.

> *Fondly,*
> *John*

March 25 66

My Darling-

I told you that Charlie had a surprised planned for us. He tried-hard. We were routed out of bed at 11 PM to standby to evac aircraft to Bien Hoa. None of us could sleep from the artillery noise anyway, so we got up and milled around for awhile before it was decided that things were OK.

What had happened was: that a bunch of V.C. in RVN clothing had walked into an RVN clothing had walked into an RVN compound south of here and captured 17 half-tracks and were thinking about coming up here for a jangle. Artillery cleaned them out long before they got up here. About 42 of them. You might have heard about it on TV or elsewhere back there. We don't get any news at all over here.

Angel-I write these things in the light that I think of them as they happen and without any relish or other garbage. But not to worry you. I have no taste for any of this at all and wish I were a lifetime away from here, aware of nothing but my wife and children around me and let the world blow itself crazy. But I'm not and have 11 months of it yet as of tomorrow, and so I'll watch it as it happens and tell you some of it once in awhile.

I took a shower early tonight and came in the tent just to sit awhile. A storm started blowing in from the south with more lightning and thunder than any of us have ever seen. I had just started this letter to you when the sky opened up and Remsberg ran in to get out of it.

Old Bob has had a few beers too many and has been sitting in here talking about the family-especially Mike. He broke down with tears in his eyes and talked it all out. It will happen to me too. As the rain increased the whole area became a lake with 4-5 inches of water. Our tent floor is higher and I'm dry. The tent next door is still being worked on and the men are sloshing around, digging under the water for tools and the humor of it has brightened Remsberg up enough so he is in spirits enough to start cutting the Army and forget his homesickness. I just discovered he got four letters home from Lois today and with pictures of the kids.

Now-to your letter Angel. I got a howl out of Doug's writing his request on the blackboard. He's earned the book already. I showed Doug's printing around to Remsberg, Ellard, and Johnson and they were genuinely amazed at how well a first grader could print. I'm very proud of Doug and know that we'll have no problem with a boy that can read and write that good.

Tell Mark that I am proud of him too-for being Mommy's helper when Doug is at school. I'm glad that the ditch incident has happened as it did and that you have placed the creek off limits unless you are there...

I've had a hard time writing this letter. Being interrupted by these happy drunks all of the time. Bob has left to wade back into his tent. (We're trying to move him down here since I moved yesterday.)

I'm going to build a desk tomorrow and then maybe I can start writing decent letters-instead of on my lap.

Tomorrow is one month off the tour Angel. I'm working on a deal to meet you in Hawaii for two weeks in August- I hope it works. Don't get your hopes up to high. Yet its something to plan for. O.K.?

> *Kiss my boys and tell them I will write soon.*
> *Sweet dreams to you tonight my own, sweet love.*

> > > *John*

> > > *March 27*
> > > *Phu Loi*

My Darling-

> *I received #7 from you today...*

> *As usual, your letters are the highlight of the whole day and I store them away very carefully, to be read over again.*

> *Yesterday, I went to Saigon with the Supply Officer on a scrounge run and came back empty handed. We need lumber up here something fierce. The C.O. and OPS O. flew and we took 2 jeeps along inside the ship for transport on arrival.*

> *Saigon must have been a pretty city once upon a time. Now its crowded to the breaking point and fierce with traffic. The Saigon office warriors live well down there in government rented homes and hotels and we were a sharp contrast to them in our sweat and mud soaked fatigues.*

> *We ate lunch on the roof patio of a large hotel along with these soft living thugs. War is hell down there. I heard one Colonel complaining about his air-conditioner not working for 2 whole hours. Tough.*

> *Last night when we got back I scrounged 17 large USAF Type Wall lockers and handed them out for people to share-keeping one for myself. It took almost all day finding screws to assemble mine and in the heat putting it all together really pooped me. But now I have most of my stuff stored neatly and maybe tomorrow I can build a small desk for myself. I hope that all this labor is not in vain. It could very well be because very soon now, we are going to be forced to trade 15 pilots with the 1st CAV up north. Shields will have to put names in a hat and pull out the unlucky ones. So who knows where I'll be in a week or so?*

> *I'm in better shape now. Most of my heat rashes are gone and my blisters have cleared up. The only good thing about this*

place is the water-here it is soft and delicious as opposed to Saigon and Vung Tau. I probably drink 2-and-a-half-3 gallons a day up here.

Your #7 letter apologized for a blue and sad letter-that I haven't received yet. Whatever it has to say, there is no need to apologize princess. If we can communicate and stay in tune with each other just as we do when we are together, then we aren't so very apart in spirit. And as long as we are close in heart- then we are still faithful to our vows.

I WILL write my boys-soon. Its just that now, I am very tired and sore and things happening and changing so fast each day, that I haven't caught up with myself yet.

I must close now and try to sleep this night. I love you, I love you, I love you.

Sweet dreams-John

March   28, 1966
My Darling-

I stood in the heat of the HQ Tent at noon, long enough to find some mail from you.

The heat baked every tent here like an oven from 10:00 AM until our second big rain of monsoon season started at 2:00 PM. I have never heard or seen anything like it before-much heavier than the last one a few days ago and still nothing compared to what is to come. The thunder was so loud that we had to cover our ears to ease the pain from the noise. Again, the area turned into a lake and the floor of the tent was only an inch above water-and we built it 10 inches above ground. I took some pictures of people out in it after I got to the tent and changed clothes. Tents blew down and personal possessions and gear submerged or floated away. Now at 8:30PM the area is half-drained and a sea of mud. One man killed a snake over 5 feet long that swam into his tent. Consequently, I accomplished little work at all today in the Motor Pool-and could care less.

I went over your two letters several times today and tried-with ease to imagine my family doing the events that you so described so nicely.

I'm very happy that you went to the zoo and that it was an enjoyable visit for you. Doing these things with the boys in a relaxed mood is a good tonic for all of you and it warms me to vision my bride and boys happy together in these things.

I overheard a conversation outside the tent just before I started this letter that might interest you. A Mr. Jones, the Far East Boeing-Vertol Boss-who was at Alameda that day I left, has just arrived in the area for a visit. He was talking about the unit and his trip and he said that the day the carrier left he saw one of the 178th Officers saying goodbye to his family at the pier. He told this 11th Battalion Officer he had seen a lot of goodbyes lately, but watching that family and those two small boys was something especially touching to him. I was inside, taking off my boots and remained silent about it-he will recognize me soon enough any way...

I'm going to sign off at this point tonight my beautiful one-to write Doug and Mark a few lines before I try again for some sleep. I missed you next to me very much last night. I will hold you in my arms again tonight hoping that your are safe and warm together.

I love you-infinity John

MARCH 28
PHU LOI

DEAR BOYS:

HOW ARE YOU/ I HOPE YOU ARE SAFE AND HAPPY. I HOPE YOU OBEY MOMMY AND STAY AWAY FROM THE CREEK. I HOPE YOU ARE CAREFULL IN THE STREET.

MOMMY SENT ME SOME OF DOUG'S PRINTING. IT WAS BETTER THAN I DO AND I AM PROUD. I AM PROUD ABOUT A LOT OF THINGS. I AM PROUD THAT YOU BOYS WENT ON THE BUS ALL BY YOURSELVES. DID YOU HAVE A

*GOOD TIME AT GRANDPA AND GRANDMA'S HOUSE? I AM
PROUD THAT DOUG WANTS A NEW BOOK. I HOPE THAT
MARK LIKES TO HAVE DOUG READ TO HIM. HOW DO YOU
LIKE YOUR NEW SCHOOL HAT DOUG?*

*MOMMY SAYS THAT YOU HAD A GOOD TIME AT THE
ZOO.*

*TELL MOMMY THAT SHE IS PRETTY FOR ME AND
REMEMBER THAT SHE IS A LADY AND YOU SHOULD TAKE
TURNS PULLING OUT HER CHAIR FOR HER AT THE TABLE
AT HOME AND WHEN YOU ARE OUT FOR DINNER.*

*I KNOW MY BOYS ARE THE BEST IN THE WHOLE
WIDE WORLD AND THAT IS WHY I AM VERY PROUD.*

*PLEASE REMEMBER TO TELL MOMMY THAT I LOVE
HER WHEN SHE PUTS YOU TO BED TONIGHT AND ALL OF
YOU HAVE-*

SWEET DREAMS   DADDY

30 March 1966
Phu Loi

My Darling-
*I didn't write last night because I was putting the shelves
together for my scrounged wall locker. It took four hours of sweat.*

*Rain again last night and a cool 74 degrees this morning at
dawn. Not for long though. It was 105 inside the tent by 2PM
today-and not a breeze anywhere*

*The #11 letter arrived yesterday. Thank you so much Alice
and you too boys. Daddy will be thinking of all of you with a
special love on April 10th. The only present I want- is to know that
my beloved family is safe and happy...*

*Your mention of Mark sitting outside patiently unwinding
string touched me very deeply-as it was like that with me, watching
him on his "T" Bird on the day before I left. Oh God, how I love
them. I have refused to look at the pictures in my wallet of you and
the boys. But by accident, I see Doug's latest school snap once in*

awhile and I cannot bear to look-yet. Soon enough will come the time when I want to dwell on pictures that you send me. But until then I want to put it off as much as is possible because the hurt is too great now.

We had our bad day yesterday. Shields had to pick those people that would have to go to the 1st CAV up north- 10 of them. So at 4PM he pulled names out of a hat and read off the slips of paper. I didn't make it and was relieved. Yet Remsberg's name got called. They will leave on the 16th for AN KHE. I was very sorry about Bob and we went to the little tent we call a bar-where I left him an hour later

At 11PM last night he came stomping in the tent-shouting like hell and pretty drunk-along with some of the others who have to go. I woke up and sat and talked with him for awhile before he decided to go to bed.

Tomorrow- we begin our flying operations here-in a big exercise.

Will you please send me Ron Rodgers address in Texas and Mike Deegan's in Alabama if you have it somewhere?

Tell me how you are doing without me Alice- in everything. I don't desire a woman as such at all and haven't since I left-and I damned sure don't expect to either.

But I do miss and want YOU terribly.

I love you   John

March 31, 1966

My Darling-
........I went flying this morning-getting a DECCA Checkout. Really something. It is a system of position plotting yourself and has a running strip map on a roller in the cockpit. Hell, I could have flown into Cambodia and never have known it, for all I know about the area over here so far. A civilian representative is over here checking us out in it and he lives in the tent with us. He knows the country very well.

We had a break today- no rain and a high cloud cover that kept the temperature down. The best day we have had yet.

I took a blow today. We have to move the Motor Pool-after all the work the men did to set it up-now Bn wants it moved. I raised hell and let it be known that the Colonel had some real idiots working for him.

One good break today. My boots that I special ordered in the States aren't worth a hill of beans. I've been walking-or limping around on bleeding blisters for a week now. The older boots have started to fall apart from wearing them each day-dry rot. Dave Clark-the Supply Officer got me 2 new pairs of Jungle Boots. So maybe I will have relief in a few days.

We have a Mama-San for the tent now. All she does is the laundry so far. No sweeping or shining of boots. Its hard to get Vietnamese help since their afraid to work here because of V.C. retribution. Anyway her name is Mai-something or other, and knows about five words of English: OK, NO, WASHY, YOU, SOAP. Its really a riot trying to get back our own laundry and I have told her one more foul up and I'll give her over to the V.C.

She understood and didn't show up for work yesterday. Today she peeked around to see if I was in the tent before she'd come in. She'll learn our ways soon enough I guess. Not a bad gal- a war widow.

I cant get used to the ones they have hired to work in the mess tent. These pajama clothes they wear make me think I'm eating three breakfasts a day. Keep thinking of you running around the house in the morning...

Mierhoffer just moved into the tent having been flying with the 147th at Vuang Tau. The artillery going off around here has got him all shook up and he's worried about the V.C. coming in here. It would take 4000 men to breach the perimeter- if they wanted to die for it. They can have it if they want it-after I leave here.

Well, lover-I'll close this one and mail it tonight and wonder how all of you are tonight.

Kiss them for me and snuggle yourself tight.

Sweet dreams   John

2 April

My Darling-

 I usually get my letters started to you before as late an hour as this (10PM) but we had a tent gripe session tonight and it has just ended.

 We became operational today and I started accepting missions. I caught a flight down to Saigon and went into Finance to my March pay. I am keeping $150 a month and sending the rest to you.... Save all you can Angel, as I intend to do over here. All I can see right now, is you and me together in Hawaii for 10-11 days in August-that is what I go to sleep on every night.

 Yet something much bigger is in the mill for us. Unless I change my mind- or the situation changes in world events-and I don't expect that it will. I intend to leave the service when I return. Just how and when depends on where I have orders to return to the U.S. It will mean a large loss in pay-and maybe even no pay for awhile-but we'll make out somehow.

 I have decided that you need a husband and the boys need a father worse than we need this kind of life we are living now. I don't plan on ever leaving my family again on a trip like this one. They can have the whole 12 years and jam it...

 I sure hope you don't get mosquitoes there when summer comes. Its summer all year here and the rainy season has started now. The place never really dries up and pools of stagnant water breed these mosquitoes something fierce. They are especially bad here in the tent tonight.

 Last night before dark I flew a Jeep up to LAI KHE to get it fixed up from an accident at an ordnance outfit. LAI KHE AIRSTRIP is cut out off trees at the bottom of the Michelin Rubber Plantation and all the units there are tented in the trees. Green and cool and very beautiful. I saw several old French plantation houses and one beautiful one with large veranda's, rooms, and so on. Really something out of the old 'Terry and the Pirates." It is now HQ for a brigade commander in the 1st INf. DIV....

3 April

My Darling-

    Today I flew on one of our first operational missions. Nothing hard-really, but after we had been gone ten hours and had logged only 5 hours and ten minutes I was whipped. It is a struggle simply to fly in the heat and dust. The carrying of personal armor, survival gear, canteen, helmet, maps and etc. into the cockpit is in itself, a staggering task. To climb into the cockpit over and around the "Iron Maiden" exhausts one completely. The "Iron Maiden" is an armor sheath that locks over the body after entrance into the seat. Opened, it makes cockpit entrance almost impossible. Once closed, it makes availability of circuit breakers (and we have hundreds, above, below, on back and on all sides) switches, levers and so on - many times impossible. It would preclude the fast- or even slow exit from the aircraft in case of a crash. Yet it is designed to protect the vital organs from at least a 30 caliber round. I will wear it closed on a combat assault for sure, but the rest of the time, to hell with it. I fly with it open.

    Today was a typical ASH & TRASH haul up to LAI KHE-only a short flight from here. We hauled CONEX containers and our total haul today was 32,070 LBS, 13 passengers, 12 sorties and one internal load of lumber that damned near ruined the whole aircraft. At the end of the day we had 4 major write-ups in the log book for maintenance people, had almost crushed our crew chief and were groggy from the radio noise.

    Radio! My God! There are so many radio transmissions going on all the time that my mind was reeling from them. Everywhere we fly we have to dodge our own artillery and the job of finding a landing zone becomes a major life-or-death matter, trying to sneak through our own fire-especially with radios that quit working at the most crucial moment.

    Since we have only now become operational, many things have to be ironed out-for months to come, before we can get things down pat. By the time we had shut down for the last time today, I had learned a life time of experience and was drenched with sweat and dust until it hurt to close my eyes- for the dirt in them.

    Yet it remains a war of contrasts.

I went to the Mess tent and picked two steaks to grill myself (a regular Sunday night affair) and had a dinner that would have cost $12 back in the States. I was too tired eat it later and came here to the tent to watch the floor for an hour and smoke cigarettes.

The rain started and I decided to get to the shower before I was flooded out of it. We use old Air Force Wing Tip tanks for our showers and the sun heats the water all day long. So I stood in the cold rain and wind, enjoying a warm shower. A lot better life than a lot of people have over here...

You wrote and asked if there was a safe place at all in Viet-Nam. No darling, there isn't anywhere at all. I'm safer here then I am with 4 people in a jeep in Saigon. The men down in the Motor Pool are on the crucial edge of our perimeter. And even though we got shot at on final approach into the airstrip, I would rather have that then sleep down by the trucks at night.

But so much for that...

Sweetheart I'm too tired to write another line. I'll sleep this night.

Infinity, John

5 April 1966

My Darling-

Another day off the tour. Hot yesterday- a long day for me where I doodled around getting personal things squared away that had been left hanging. There was a big lift yesterday, down South near Vuang Tau and everyone got back late at night. Full of war stories and etc.

I pulled a coup off against the Army. I have collected for yours and the boys travel out to California, plus dislocation allowance. We were not supposed to be able to do this because of those orders that brought us out of Alaska. Yet the Unit Movement Orders gave me an out. They may try to collect it later- but I'll fight it. In the meantime I'm going to send you an M.O. for $417. A nice little bundle to save.

Honey, I just don't know what to write to you about this damned place over here. I don't want to frighten you and when I comment on the days' activities, you cannot possibly visualize the time picture, no matter how hard I attempt to write it accurately for you.

You know the better than I do what is happening over here- with TV and etc. All we know is what rumors we hear or what we are involved in.

To be truthfull, we are involved.

The C.O. was shot down last night and got repaired and out O.K. Nobody was hurt. Today I logged 4:45 Combat Assault time and earned it- out near the Cambodian border.

So how and what else should I tell you? I sure don't know and guess the best thing is not to write anymore of it at all...

We had a movie tonight. A humor movie where the heroine ran through the whole movie in a negligee. Some Italian gal. Sure got me thinking about you and of things I should put in the back of my mind.

I must confess that I don't like to think of you that way-yet when I do, it is so very, very pleasant. And with good reason. One of these days I'm going to break down and write a torrid letter and hope to get it all out of my system for awhile. I suppose I'll feel like a base clod after I mail it-and wish that I hadn't done so- but you are YOU and the reason for all of my yearning thoughts.

You've been doing a wonderful job of writing to me about yourself and the boys- and the picture in my minds eye is not you alone- but of my whole family, as a wonderful, safe unit. Happy and secure.

The letter I received today was such as I have mentioned. Doug's letter to me that you weren't supposed to read- and Mark's precious drawing of how my place looks. Not bat at all-the little bugger.

I had better close with those kind of happy thoughts for tonight. I do love you. Kiss my boys for me-extra hard.

Sweet dreams- John

8 April
Bien Hoa

Princess-

We'll here we go again-it seems each time I leave my happy home, I wind up in the hospital.

This time it started out as a Kidney Stone. I woke put in the early hours of the 5th and thought someone had stabbed me in the side. It hurt so bad I couldn't make a sound. So I crawled and slid out of the tent, next door to operations and told the switchboard operator to feet a Medic- the next thing I knew I was here at the 93rd Med Evac at Bien Hoa. Since then-until now, at evening, I've been pretty doped up and in pain.

The doctor determined that I also have prostitus-prostrate gland infected. This compounds the situation considerably so I don't know how long I'll be in here.

The hospital is a series of Quonset hut complexes next to the airfield and is staffed by all beautiful nurses. That's all they've got is looks though because I wouldn't give a hill of beans for any of them as a nurse. I had to beg for pain pills from several of these bitches- who were busy doing their nails.

I don't want to you to worry about me at all. Don't let Dad & Ruth make any phone calls over here like last time. Just sit there at home and don't worry. O.K? I'll be O.K. soon enough.

The only problem now is getting mail sent over to me from the unit. Continue to write me at the 178th.

Tell my boys I love them and imagine a big kiss yourself from me.

Love-John

April 10
Bien Hoa

My Darling:

Easter Sunday over here is just another hot day- but I woke up thinking about all of you and believing that Easter for you will be a happy one there in the house.

There are two good nurses here-I must retract my earlier statement. One of the gals works the graveyard shift and the other the day shift. The graveyard gal woke us up with shouts of "Happy Easter!' as she shoved thermometers in our mouths.

I told her today was double-barreled for me- being my birthday...

During the day many Regimental, Battalion, and Company Commanders came here to see their respective men and wish them well. Even a Brigadier, the Asst. CG of the 25th came through handing out Purple Hearts to his people. No PIO people with him at all. A very sincere and humble old man.

We have an Australian soldier here in the ward. What a wound! He was under fire and running for cover and jumped over a log and landed with a poisoned Pungi stake right up-you know where! The medics think its a "first" in this war.

Not long after lunch I was laying in the sack all doped up with pain killers when the two Red Cross women marched by towards the nurses station. Pretty soon they came back with the nurse- singing "Happy Birthday John." They gave me a 2 LB Coffee can filled with cookies-baked by some lady in the Tokyo Embassy Club and a small Table Model Transistor Radio that runs on 3 small batteries...

When I return, the story will change somewhat. I owe my family something better than a gypsy life and no place to call home.
That is why I've made up my mind to get out. I'll be giving up a hell of a lot of good pay to do it and we'll be back at the bottom again. But at least the boys will have a more permanent establishment and you will have a home-somewhere that you can call your own...

A lot depends on where I get orders to upon return from this bloody hole. For example, if I get Fort Wolters then I'd stay in a while and get us squared away down there with a job with Southern Airways...

Well, darling-time to close another one to you and take a slug of pain killers. I sure wish I would pass this thing. Yet the time in here all counts off the tour.

> *Take care of yourselves, stay happy*
> > *Love John*

P.S. Tell Mark his picture is very good and my place looks just like he drew it. Although he should have put in some raindrops.

April 11
Bien Hoa

Angel-

"My Side Hurts" - Mark would say and hold himself while you and I would feel for him and pray and rub it away from him.

Tell Mark that Daddy knows what his sideache felt like, now. And that Daddy thinks he was a very brave boy. To tell the truth, I'm not so brave anymore now that its wearing away on me and I can imagine myself agreeing to anything if I had to for a pain killer.

I get two pain pills every four hours and when it gets too bad, a shot in the arm. I'm smoking about 3 packs a day in this place from going nuts with boredom. And still I haven't passed anything. The doctor says the more I drink water and the more I walk around, the sooner I'll pass it...

The Australian soldier here as joined by another one today- so he's not lonesome. This new one was shot in the same place. So there must be something to the saying "Down Under."

I've been wondering about the boys and Sunday school Alice. Have they expressed a desire to attend again- and have you thought about it, or picked one yet? Just wondering...

Those thoughts-and others like them sustain me darling. You must always remember and believe that the greatest treasure in my life, is my family and I owe it all to you.

Sweet dreams John

13 April 1966
Bien Hoa

My Darling-

Another wonderful letter from you today.

So the boys saw Bambi. I had thought about it coming over on the boat, but had since forgotten about it. I wish that I had been there to share it with them. I remember thinking, when Doug was very small, of all the Disney movies and that I wanted him to see them too. Bambi was foremost amongst them.

Yes, Alice I have deposited the idea of getting out of the service when I return. Reason: The way things are going now, I will have 9-12 in the States when I return before having to come back over here again. Those are the latest figures. A miracle would have to occur before anything would change that.

According to the Army Times, I was a Captain on April 6th....

Here is how the pay will stack up for me as a CAPT.

$695.00 base pay

$205.00 flight pay

$130.00 Quarters Allowance

$47.88 subsistence

$65.00 hostile fire pay

$30.00 family separation allowance

$57.70 Cost of Living Allowance (COLA)

$1230.63 Total

That's a hell of a lot of money to say goodbye to if I get out of the Army...

I had a front row seat at the USO show today-over in the next ward. DANNY KAYE and VIKKI CARR. Both very good. A clean decent show. The best I've seen overseas. I wish I had my camera with me. I didn't...

You closed your letter by saying that now that I'm flying your worried even more. Angel-if you could see the meat factory I'm in now, you'd Thank God I am flying. These infantry kids come in here all torn to hell-wiped out before they even know what hits them. I'm convinced I'm safer in the air than in my bunk. Those are the odds. I'll say goodbye to you now Princess and sweet dreams tonight. Dream of me.

I love you   John

DEAR DOUG AND MARK
DID YOU SEE BAMBI?
DID YOU LIKE IT?
WASN'T THUMPER FUNNY?
SO WAS FLOWER?
BAMBI GREW BIG AND STRONG
AND SMART AND BRAVE.

SOME BAD MAN WAS NOT CAREFULL
AND STARTED THE FORREST FIRE
BUT BAMBI SAVED SOME OF HIS FRIENDS
YEH FOR BAMBI

I LOVE YOU
DAD

April 18
Bien Hoa

Angel-
     I've just seen the doctor and I am being discharged back to duty this morning.
Yesterday and the day before were my worst days in here since I couldn't hold anything down- but then last night I came out of it and passed some 'gravel"- and the ache is gone and I feel O.K. now...

April 19 1966
Phu Loi

My Darling Wife-
     I arrived back here at PHU LOI yesterday after lunch, 18 pounds lighter than when I left and am weak as a cat but overjoyed to find these letters from Carol-and one from Ruth...

     The sad news of our 4&5 dying put tears in my eyes for all of us. I loved that little turtle too. He was part of a life of ours that I hold most dear and my heart goes out to our boys. I've written a separate letter to Mark-and Doug about 4&5-for you to read to them. I must say that I resent being away especially at times like these-where Dad should be there to ease and help with this situation but again, from what you wrote of the funeral, the cross and the prayer, I think you are fortunate to have a memory that will serve you long after our boys are grown and gone separate ways from us. Thank you for sharing it with me as beautifully as you did on paper.
     Your second letter chewed me out more than a little angel-about scaring you with Red Cross Stationary. I'm truly sorry Alice and I had no intentions to frighten you in any way. Additionally, you must believe that

I was not trying in any way to make you jealous when I mentioned beautiful nurses. I commented on it because of the oddities that prevail over here. Such as: Down at Vuang Tau the 36th MEDEVAC has wonderful facilities for a hospital- air conditioning-permanent buildings and etc.- and the most god-awfullest looking females ever seen by the human eye. Whereas the 93 MEDEVAC out in the boondocks of Bien Hoa has the bare essentials to operate with and one would not expect to see such handsome women in the midst of such squalor. Like I said before- a war of contrasts.

As far as craving your food goes-listen gal- the night I got well, I sat up all night talking with the night nurse-about your cooking and our ritual each Sunday up in Alaska and she finally asked me what I missed more; you or your cooking? Without revealing any intimate thoughts, I assured her that the lovely lady in the picture is what I missed more than anything in this world. Lord, how true it is darling.

There is an old (Chinese, I believe) saying that birds only make nests at happy houses. And your report of a bird nest for the boys to watch is another piece of warming news for me. Each time you write to tell me how happy you and the boys are there and of these small events that are big in their world, I am given an unusual sense of tranquility over how you are doing back there. I hope that it is not a false sense of security.

Now I want to write about you and me:
You signed off the last letter saying that you wished that I was there-that you would like to go to bed with me. I guess that is the first time you have written that to me and it sent an electric charge through me right down to my toes. I'll tell you this about me. I find myself not desiring sex-"as sex" at all over here. The usual Playboy pin-ups are the wall lockers, all girls with jutting breasts and smooth flat tummies-all very nice. Yet they don't bother me at all. I'm pleased to find myself comparing none against you since I don't consider you down in that class of female.

Instead, I have in my memory the vision of my own woman, my wife, all mine and with her own promise and secrets in the way she has moved with me and the intrigue of delights that I have found in and from your body- the things that you-and we- do together and to each other, are mine alone to dwell upon. So you see Alice-I don't miss sex. I MISS YOU...

Most of the time I dwell upon you (when I separate you from the children in my thoughts), it usually starts with seeing you well groomed and dressed, and the knockout you are, and how proud I am to have you at my side for the whole world to see that you are mine.

Then I see us together, comfortable and cozy sitting on the couch together- or you are curled up in a chair with your knitting or reading a book. This serene picture usually serves me well because it indicates that all is well, that the boys are in bed-safe nearby and you and I have those moments to do as we please with ourselves. If it is nothing more than occupying the same room together, it is the life with you that I found so rewarding.

Yet make no mistake about it-there isn't a night that I have gone to bed without letting myself be teased with the thought of your own body against mine...

Lastly, I admit to you that because of the thought of you, I have made-or allowed myself to 'come' twice over here. Laying in bed, bone-tired and thinking of you, I have let my hand hold it-and shut my eyes extra hard and imagined it was you that was touching me. A mess was made and I had to use my 'T' shirt, but the memory of my wife is that vivid honestly and honestly, I don't feel a bit guilty about it at all. Instead, I feel proud that I feel that strongly about you-rather than "sex alone."

I hope I have made myself clear to you darling. If there is anything that I should feel guilty about-or if I have offended you, please write me and say so.

An added note: Please send me your 3 Bean Salad recipe for two reasons. 1. The Mess Hall is enthusiastic about it 2. The nurses at the 93rd went wild just thinking about it when I described it to them. I hope you didn't mind my bragging about it to them.

I will follow this letter with a letter to our boys about 4 & 5.

April 19 1966

Dear Mark-and Doug too-

Mommy wrote to me the sad news about 4&5. I was so sorry to hear that I cryed a daddy's tears because I love 4&5 too. Mark 4&5 was your turtle and pet and I understand how much it hurts you inside when you loose something you love. I was so very sorry for you Mark-and if you cried tears for 4&5 then it shows that you loved your little pet- or else it wouldn't have hurt you so much. So don't ever be ashamed to cry tears for something you love.

Doug I am saying these words to you too-because I know that you loved 4&5 just as much as "greeny and you were sorry to see 4&5 die.

Mommy wrote me that you decided to have a funeral for 4&5 and that she made a little cross for the grave-and that my boys did that for a loved pet makes me very proud of my sons and it shows that you boys are learning that there are sad things that happen to us in our lives too.

Mommy writes that you will have a second 4&5 Mark and I know you will love it just as much as our first 4&5. So Mark-and you too Doug, I want you boys to be happy that the first 4&5 was yours as long as he was alive and he lived in a happy home.

4&5 was getting sick and it was God's way of being kind to him to let him die instead of being sicker and sicker and not feeling well. So you should feel good that 4&5 was taken away to God in heaven where he will be happy instead of sick here on Earth.

Daddy had lots of pets when he was a little boy-that died. And each time, Daddy cried for awhile and then found other happy things to think about-and I know you will too.

Thats about all I have to say Mark-and Doug. I just wanted to let you know that I feel the same way you do even though I am far away from you.

I love you both very much-and always will. Be good to each other and sleep tight each night with many sweet dreams.

Love Daddy

April 23 1966
Phu Loi

Angel-

I received a letter from you yesterday and avoided answering it until now, strictly because there just wasn't any news to write about...

I am still grounded-because I've got a racking cough and am weak- but I should be flying in a few more days. Until I do fly, I'll be acting C.O. since starting tomorrow the unit will be involved in a GRF out at Tay Ninh called "Operation Birmingham." You'll probably be reading about it back there.

Everyone will be gone on this one and the operation is supposed to last two weeks. So when I do go, mail from me will probably be sporadic at best-for awhile.

C.O. Shields walked in the tent after lunch and handed me some Captains bars and a set of orders. My date of rank is 8 April. So now I'll address my mail as Captain. Thank you for saying you are proud of me- I know you mean it.

Your phone calls must have done your spirits some good. I'll try to boost them too- one of these days with a phone call to you from Saigon USO. Three minutes will cost $6.00. Don't know when I'll get the chance, but it will be as soon as I can get down there.

Thats about it for tonight Angel.

Sweet Dreams   John

April 24 1966
Phu Loi

Angel-

....The area is all but deserted, with everyone out near the border on the first day of this operation. I treated the company enlisted men to a one hour beer bust for my promotion last night- figuring they deserved it more than anyone else- and in one hour they went thru about 25 cases of beer! I drank one beer...

Mama-San brings in our Mama-Sans and shows them the family picture-and they jabber away excitedly with one another pointing to you and the boys-and then all nod to me and say: "Number One." That's a very high compliment from these emotionless and humorless people.

Its 105 here in the tent again- and my liquid diet of late consists of: Rose's Lime Juice, ice and Quinine water-sometimes laced with a shot of Gin. I usually start that about noon and have 5 or 6 before supper time.

I wonder what you are doing? Enjoy that air-conditioning all you can Angel. And tonight pretend I'm there with my head at your breasts with my hands around your waist.

I love you
John

April 26, 1966
Phu Loi

My Darling Wife:

I received no mail from you today, unusual. I did receive a letter from Carol-nice and newsy. She told me about "Doug Duck and Duck," the ducks they bought for the kids...

I will receive a full month of Captain's pay plus 23 days of this month as a Captain...now I can just see your eyes sparkle at the thought of all this money coming your way. It will make you the best dressed widow in the area...

You can see that there is a lot of income to give up if I get out of the Army upon my return. But what the hell have we saved so far-running around the globe? And I'm convinced that this war is going to be a 10-15 year affair over here in S.E. Asia. And if I thought I could get a 2-and-a-half or 3 year tour with my family before returning over here again-I might change my thinking about it. But it does not look that way to me.

I wrote Smithey a long letter yesterday and asked him what the current thinking and prospects were for a man in my situation. I also told him of my plans to leave the service-unless he could convince me that this situation is going to improve...a lot of what I do angel, is how you feel about all of this. How you feel about starting all over again after 10 years of marriage and some real responsibilities (like two boys) gained along the way. There isn't a day that goes by that I dont think about it-and our future. So search your soul Alice-and I have and continue to do each day. And come up with your true feelings. I know you would stick by me through thick and thin and that your real test of this is how you manage yourself while I am here with filthy savages trying to kill me each day. But think beyond now and try to see us starting all over again and its affect on you-and thereby the both of us...

So far, I've received 25 letters from you. I'll be looking for #26 tomorrow.
Until then.

Sweet dreams angel.
Love   John

April 27 1966
Phu Loi

My Darling-
...Of all your descriptive narratives I have read thus far, none has touched me so deeply-nor made me long for the sight and touch of all of you-as much as did your description of our son Doug walking to and home from school, Yes, I believe that he sang most of the way and stopped to sit down to look at his books-my precious first born son. How I long to hold him in my arms and watch his innocent eyes as he seeks the answers to all of his curiosity about his world around him. These moments that we can spy on their world make us fortunate thieves as innocent as them and we are cleansed of any of the worldly knowledge that makes us adult-and sadder for it. Steal every moment you can of these golden years with them my love, for there is nothing so dear in our roles as parents as these rewards...

I will return to flying status tomorrow and leave here for an overnight stay up at Tay Ninh, where all the action is. The plan is for every other night back here at the company area. Sleeping in the aircraft is no fun but it beats what the infantry has to do.

Had a hell of a time with Mama-San today and finally had to get an interpreter. Somehow, she got it from the other Mama-Sans that I had said she was No. 10 thereby loosing face and causing much weeping and wailing. The more she cried, the louder I shouted until it was a standoff. I finally got it straightened out and was physically exhausted by it all. Really a mess with a bunch of women all standing around pitching in and me outnumbered.

I see that my handwriting has improved on this government stationary, so I think I'll stick to it. Good for writing the boys on too.

I guess I'll sign off for now my love and pack my bags for tomorrow. Sleep tight and tuck them in for me my darling.

I love-infinity John

April 29 1966
Phu Loi

My Darling-
 I got up at 5:00AM today and took off at 5:40, to arrive back here at 7:00PM. A long day. I can't remember being so filthy in years. The entire interior of the ship had a half-inch of dirt and grit in it-and I was no exception. No letter tonight, yesterday either, so I went to chow and came back and stood in our outside shower for a half an hour. Then I came back and laid down on the bed for a few hours. Can't sleep because of all the stories being swapped about the day's activities. The more the booze, the louder and greater the stories.
 Our ship hauled 30 tons of ammo, howitzers, and cargo today in the greatest and most unorganized mess I've ever seen in my life. It sure would be nice if we could have an enemy as fouled up as the U.S. Army.
 I didn't write last night because the Chaplain, who was also a patient in the hospital when I was there dropped by for a chat- and stayed late.
 I have written Rodgers and Deegan about jobs at their respective location and wrote Carol, asking that Jim send me a study guide for the commercial pilots written exam. Additionally, I wrote Smithey, stating my intentions and asking some questions about current Army plans. So you can see what direction I am moving towards.
 I feel so far away from all of you tonight-in a life so different from anything you have ever imagined. I miss all of you and the joy and the laughter that is ours over the little things. My boys? How are they acting for you? Is anything getting you down? Can you make it alone for another 10 months without me? Will you have changed when I return? Will anything ever be the same? These things I think about tonight-and I think about all of the time but once in a while, they overwhelm me and I know that I will not sleep tonight-thinking about them. When I return, I will never leave you again. I should have made this decision years ago-but didn't. Forgive me.
 I love you   John

April 30 1966

My Darling-

    Another day like yesterday. We didn't get back here until 9:00PM and were just as crudy as yesterday. We'll be out again tomorrow and the next day-and the next. You won't be hearing the truth about this "Operation Birmingham" back there. Its out in "war Zone C' and we were landing in areas about an half-mile from the Cambodian border. Hell for all I know we were in Cambodia a couple of times. The rest of it is combat stories and I wouldn't know where to start-so I won't.

    Anyway, I came back too damned tired to care about anything-until I saw my mail in my pidgeon hole in the OPS tent. A letter and package of photos. I ate some cold chow and had a colder shower and then sat down with my mail.

    My darling- I can't tell you how warmed and pleased I was with your news about early Sunday services and Sunday school. Your remarks about Doug and Mark took me there right along your side and I could picture every bit of it...

    The pictures were the greatest thing that has happened to me yet. Lord, they were just what I needed and I treasure every one of them. As soon as I have a chance, I will put them up in my wall locker. But for now, I will enjoy the simple act of just leafing thru them time and time again. Here is one very good picture of you and them-with the boys and their birthday cake. Your always neat and clean looking-as the boys are. Thank God you cannot see me now. Just keep living in that wonderful world-the voices of our children, clean sheets, water, hot food, FM radio and contentment-and write me about it as you have been. For you and our sons are the only link I care to maintain with that world. I miss the soft touch of your skin this night- and a bedtime story for my boys. Sweet dreams to all of you.

                      I love you darling - John

May 1, 1966
Phu Loi

My Darling, beautiful Wife-
Today I was lucky enough to be scheduled as A/C recovery
standby. We keep a ship each day for that- to sling load Huey's
that are disabled back to their base. So it meant quiet and restful
morning. Yet at noon we had to take the relief crews out to Tay
Ninh and with 32 witnesses on board I finally had my first incident
since I've been flying. I taxied the plane into a radio antenna
complex at the edge of the runway and chewed up 3 aft blades.
Lucky no one outside was hurt by flying pieces. It hurt my pride
though. After years of going into tight area and never a scratch-
then something like this in broad daylight. Did about $43,000
damage. To hell with it.

After laying around the airstrip out there, we finally caught
a ride back to Base and I was really surprised to find a letter here
for me.. Two-two days in a row...

Now, get this: I have requested 15 days leave on the
following dates- 8 to 22 August. Until you hear otherwise, plan on
that. Its only three months away so find out all you can now and let
me know so if we have to or want to change-we can-the place and
dates.

Also-honey, as soon as you have the chance, I would like
you to airmail me a certain magazine. I'm not sure of the name but
it publishes a monthly issue and an annual. The annual can be
bought throughout most of the year and that is the one I am
interested in. Its called Writers Guide or something like that. So,
see what you can do will you? Thanks...

Anyway thank you for being you and giving me the good
feeling inside when I write to you- the only girl in my world.

I love you
John

May 5 1966
Saigon

Angel-

I arrived here in the 3rd Field Hospital yesterday morning and was admitted before lunch. The doctor examined me all over and pronounced me- "A well developed, physically fit, prime male specimen." No apparent cause for these puny spells of mine and they are running a series of Lab tests on me. He guesses at heat fatigue until something else proves him wrong. I don't agree but will wait and see. The hospital is first class and just like stateside. They show outside movies next to the ward and last night was an Ann Margaret flick...

Well, another change on our trip now. After doing some talking around I've come back to the idea of Hawaii again-over all others. Herb Kraus, who I knew in Korea, is in our tent and was stationed there before orders brought him out to Benning. He recommends many things about the big island and suggests a week in a nice hotel-and then one week on the Army recreational beach on the other side of Pearl Harbor. According to Herb, the cabins are rustic and nice with a full kitchen layout and etc. This way I could spoil you for a week with Room Service, maids, flowers-wining and dining and all the things worthy of a queen, and then we could be as alone as we desire-roughing it in the sense of the word. Sound good to you? Your the one that it is for remember-I could core less where it is as long as I can see you happy and on a real honeymoon-which I never did give you and for which I've always felt cheap for.

I have enclosed the outside of yesterday's STARS & STRIPES- the first I've seen in a long time. Two articles I have marked- the one about the crew chief has all pilots talking-and for my money- he should get the Medal of Honor. He won't, but he should. I witnessed the Annotated part of the feature article from the air and on the ground. We were the only Chinook in that jungle clearing when it happened and watched the artillery we had hauled in, level their guns and fire point-blank into the woods. The AF jets were coming in directly over where the artillery shells were exploding and dropping their ordnance. I still don't why they weren't hit by our people or how they avoided the trees in all that smoke-they were that close. Needless to say, I got the hell out of there as soon as we had dumped our load of ammo.

Can't think of anything else to write to you about today Angel. There is a Korean Sgt. in the bed next to me with jungle rot on his feet and needs some help anyway. So I'll sign off for now with my prayers for your safety and security back there-please drive carefully.   *I love you-Infinity John*

May 8, 1966
Saigon

My Angel-
.....The doctor gave me a pass out of the hospital and I caught a cycle-taxi to downtown Saigon. A real teeming mess of a city. My objective was the USO where phone calls can be made to the States. I wanted to try and telephone you on Mother's Day. I didn't get there until 11:00AM and was told there were all booked up for the day. So another disappointment. I walked around and saw some bronze work and some paintings that I know we would enjoy and intend to pursue the hunt further at my next opportunity. I ate a tremendous club sandwich at the top of the Brinks Hotel and watched the Saigon warriors idle their time away. But I found myself pooped after lunch and so I returned here early in the afternoon and slept until dinner.

Well another bomb has been dropped on our Hawaii plans. The word from the unit is that all leaves to Hawaii have been cancelled until further notice. This really has me jumping mad and intend to go clear to the top to fight it. The reason seems to be: several people have gone to Hawaii and then in turn taken flights to L.A. or S.F. One Captain was caught and court-martialed.

You can assist me from that end by doing the following: Find out exactly who the Congressman is (Senator) from our area. Also who is the House of Representatives. This can be done by calling some office in Sacramento. I don't know which I should write to in the case-but California is our home state and we pay taxes there. Once I get this info from you-full name and Wash D.C. address and which party D. or R.-I intend to write to him and raise holly hell about the whole thing. My argument will be that I intend to have my wife join me in Hawaii and therefore no intent to get to the mainland can be implied. Furthermore, we would be spending money on U.S. soil and won't contributing to the Gold outflow that happens each time someone visits Hong Kong or Tokyo

I am serious about this Alice-I intend to raise as much hell as I need to and couldn't care less about the after effects . . . .

There is one way I could get to the States on a 30 day leave-emergency. All I have to do is get word from you or someone that you are out running around or that you are leaving the children to run off with someone. That is a sure fire winner to get home for 30 days. No comment.

There isnt any news to write about Angel- this hospital is wearing away at my nerves and patience like a water on a stone. Yet I just don't have any strength to move more than a short walk. They have completed just about all the tests they can perform-and all came out negative.

Sure hope someone brings me some mail tomorrow.

Kiss my boys for their Daddy and snuggle tight with me tonight in your dreams.

I love you John

May 10 1966
Saigon

Angel-

Still in the hospital-no word from the doctor. Next on the list is thyroid test.

I received quite a bit of mail from you today-one letter from Ruth telling me how much Doug and Mark enjoyed the visit to Grandmas. She left some of it to be filled in by you but she did tell me how thrilled she was to have her grandchildren there with her. After reading through yours and her letters, I was very happy for our boys and know that they wont forget about it for a long time.

You mentioned your letter writing. No Angel, I am in no way disappointed in the amount of mail I get from you. I would never want it to be a drudge or chore for you. I welcome each word I read and your easy prose conducts me along with you-in your daily household events and special happenings with the boys. I think that your furniture buying project is wise indeed since you have a lot of time and choice in the matter. Please remember to satisfy your tastes and dont worry about mine.

- Yes, Princess, I did mean AAA-and come to think of it- I received the card in the mail from you but didn't associate it with the dues in my mind.

I received your second letter-in answer to a tired and blue one that I wrote and I must say Alice, that from the way you have expressed yourself to me in letters since I have been over here, you have matured into a full woman with direction and purpose in your life. Perhaps some of it is due to the atmosphere of independence and comfortable living you enjoy this time as opposed to the last go around while I was in Korea.

I fully appreciate the fact that you are trying your best each day with the boys and that it must be very hard on you at times, being both mother and father to them. I believe every word you say when you state that their life is your life and that without them you would be lost. I know that without any of us-the others would be lost and that is how-and why my worries crop up at intervals.

As for your own behavior- I dont know how to mention it without opening an old wound. Yet I would be lying if I did not mention to you that the temptation and opportunity is there for you whenever things become too much of a burden-or your nerves scream to you for release from the day-in-day-out life that you live now. You are the target Alice for any one that men in their progressive weakness- nowadays are prone to prey on any woman, alone or otherwise who without realizing it, reveal their loss of a man around. Those that you come in daily- or occasional contact with harmless looking or not- need only the slightest encouragement before they move in closer to feel the lay of the land. I have discussed all of this with you before-at length, much to your embarrassment and impatient grief. And I wonder how much of it sunk in. 9 and-a-half months is a long time for you and that is why I want us to have a chance to be together-alone for awhile. I believe in your good intentions- as I did before. As you did too. We

*have survived a rough period in our lives that not to many can
negotiate. Nobody comes out of it without permanent scars. You
and I are no exceptions. But we have made it thus far and with
some very hard guts- we can come through this one without the
disaster that would make us just another two pieces of our own
disgust and pity. I love you-our boys, our life together as we try to
live it and I give to you-my word, that I trust you and have full
confidence in you.*

*The world, the more I see of it- is a sloped sidewalk where
millions travel in attempt to get their goal. Yet this canted walkway
leads so many toward the streetside and then into the gutter. Once
in a while, someone misses a step and gets one foot in the gutter
but managed to get back on the sidewalk where the busy crowd is
trying to push you back in and those down there already are eager
for company. So none of it is easy and each step-day by day must
be taken carefully. If we can walk hand in hand then our trip is
that much easier.*

*So now-far away from you, all I can offer instead of my
hand-is my heart, across the miles. I tried to do that before but it
was not enough. It is still offered to you but this time I believe that
you are walking on the window shopping side of the walk and are
shopping in your heart for the good things that can be had when
we-together again, reach the end of the street. So if you ask me if I
trust you-I say yes. Yet I do not trust the helping hands that are
offered to you by others-for they are oily and grimy with the stench
of the world. Enough said tonight.*

I love you-infinity   John

May 11, 1966

My Darling-

*By now the news in the States has probably revealed to you
that a Chinook crashed 110 miles north of Saigon taking a total of
21 lives. It was one of the 147's down at Vuang Tau and was
hauling replacement troops and 81 MM Mortar ammo on board.
Witnesses say it exploded in mid-air which lead me to believe that
the ammo had something to do with it. The pilots, George Clark +
John Eddy were old friends of mine.*

Then yesterday, another Chinook from the 147th crashed on the way up to Phu Loi-killing 3 passengers of 13 on board. The two pilots survived by a miracle one of them is a patient here in the hospital. There is enough left of the wreckage to allow the accident board to determine what caused the accident. I mention the above because I suspect that you will be hearing the news back in the States. It was a sad note to read your news of Frank Roop. I had not heard it over here at all.

The remainder of this letter is just enclosures. Pieces of news that I thought would be of interest to you. The card/flower and handkerchief was a gift from the wife of the VN Army Chief of Staff. She came through today with her entourage and passed these out among the patients. Sort of a Madame Nhu type character-yet very lovely and gracious with a great amount of charm and poise about her. I had just awakened and had no idea of who she was-and mumbled a few words of thanks while all of these American and VN generals stood around smiling.

The doctor is letting me out on pass tomorrow-early at about 6:00AM-so that I can get down to the USO and be there when they open at 7:00AM- to book a call to you there in the U.S. The limit I can talk is 5 minutes and will cost about $10. So here's hoping you are home all day tomorrow and tomorrow night.

Nothing else is news-so I will sign off now with my love to all of you.

I love you   John

May 12 1966
Saigon

My Darling Wife
This is the day that I talked to you on the telephone. There are no words to tell you how good it was to hear your voice-the boys voice. It did me a world of good and my spirits have lifted to the stars.

We had a bad connection- I know- but I could understand you very well although I am sorry to say that I could not understand what my boys said to me at all. I pretended as though I could and so you must write me right away what they said to me as best as you can remember-so that I can reply to them as soon as possible. Lord it was good hearing you my love and I'm glad I got up early at 5:00AM and got down to the USO long before they opened at 7:00AM-because I was fourth in line and followed by about 50 people...

I think I have spent my last trip in Saigon, it is a dirty filthy place crowded with the dregs of Viet Nam...

Once again Angel- thank God I caught you home and heard your voice and my baby boys. The next time I phone-will hope for a better connection...

I love you sweet voice John

May 15 1966
Saigon

My Darling Wife-

Still in the hospital and am now out of the care of the M.D. Hold on to your seat because here comes some news. I have LEPROSY. Just kidding there, thought it would brighten your day a little...

I am now in the care of the "Bug doctor"-'The Eleventh Hour' type. After one talk with him, his first observations are that I could be pooped from the medications taken while in the 93rd Med Evac and/or I am in a situation I don't like over here. Meaning that I have been used to being in command of my own situation and of things, and now in a Chinook outfit I am not an aircraft commander and my system does not take to sitting in the other seat and pushing switches and etc. at someone else's desires. Hell, I don't know, maybe he's got something there. It could possibly mean that I would transfer to some Huey unit and fly a gunship where I could take out my frustrations by being able to pull a trigger and have the chance to shoot back at Charlie instead of just sitting there in a Chinook like a sitting duck. I don't mean to worry you with all of this gab-but feel you have every right know what's going on.

Mark's little letter was precious and I wish I could hold him in my arms. Also, many times I think of how I would pick our big Doug up and he would wrap his legs around me as soon as he was

off the floor-and look at me with those big blue eyes of his.....
My love to all of you-especially my dream girl.

Love   John

May 16, 1966

DEAR DOUG AND MARK-
    I AM WRITING THIS NOW TO SEND YOU SOME
THINGS.
    WHEN I WAS IN DOWNTOWN IN SAIGON, WAITING TO
TELEPHONE YOU, A YOUNG LADY OFFERED ME AN OLD
PIECE OF MONEY SHE HAD.
    THIS IS VERY OLD AND WAS USED BY THE FRENCH
BEFORE INDO-CHINA WAS DIVIDED UP AND THE
COUNTRY OF VIET NAM WAS MADE. THIS HAPPENED IN
ABOUT 1953 or 1954 LONG BEFORE EITHER OF YOU WERE
BORN.
    HERE IN THE HOSPITAL WITH ME ARE SOME
AUSTRALIAN SOLDIERS. THEY ARE SENDING YOU THEIR
KIND OF STAMPS USED TO MAIL LETTERS. I THINK THAT IS
NICE OF THEM. DOUG YOU CAN USE THE MONEY FOR
SHOW AND TELL AT SCHOOL.
    THAT IS ALL FOR NOW.
    I LOVE YOU BOTH VERY MUCH-TAKE CARE

LOVE   DADDY

May 17, 1966
Saigon
Viet-Nam

My Darling Wife
    Today I have some further news to report to you. First I
want to say I received a reply from Mike Deegan in answer to my
request for information about a job at Rucker....
    This is Tuesday-on Thursday I am being evacuated to
Japan for further examination. Nothing to serious I assure you.
They simply feel that the facilities there here have not been
sufficient to complete the exams they desire. Furthermore, a more
complete staff is there to handle the job. The doctor estimates that

I should be there about 10 days before returning back here. I will continue to write to you from there but will have my unit hold your letters to me- up at Phu Loi until I return.

About the bombing in Saigon- I believe that was the day before I went downtown to phone you and the MP's were busy as hell for several days afterwards. The gate guard at the Hospital emptied several clips into some suspicious trucks that lingered a little to long out in front. All he shot up was some black market American whiskey. Hell,, Saigon is no sanctuary and the V.C. can pull something off just about any time they want to a suicide affair. Thursday-the 19th is HO CHI MINH's birthday and I expect they'll try something then too.

As far as "Operation Birmingham" goes- or went. It was a failure in the amount of V.C. killed as opposed to the loss of Americans. The big thing about it is that the storage and training areas of the V.C. has been damaged quite extensively-hospitals, schools, training areas- all of it underground and he will be hurting when the monsoon gets here-its almost here now-and months from now when troops move down the HO CHI MINH trail in from Cambodia and have no base camp to operate from, in that respect, it was a success...

Regards to my comment on a way to come home on a compassionate- about you carrying on with the garbage man sort of thing, I mentioned it only because that is how desperate the situation is over here as far as getting home. I did not mean to hurt you Alice...

I love you-stay my own size 34 will you   John
P.S. I HAVE LEPROSY OF THE PENIS

May 20 1966
Clark AFB
Phillipine Islands

My Darling Wife
*   The last letter I wrote to you- a confused and rather a mess, was written on the 18th corrected and mailed on the 19th.*

I will try to fill you in on what has happened since then.
Nothing new really. Everything is going as planned except that it is
a slow grind.

The unit packed my TW uniform and some extra shorts and
Herb Kraus flew them down to me. They also brought me my small
portable radio and the small snap of you and the family- which I
kept right here in my writing folder. The crazy bastards also
included a full bottle of Gin in my B-4 bag and spent my last night
in the 3rd Field drinking "Salty Dogs"-Pineapple Juice-Gin and
Salt, with another patient- a Lt. Col. who had a heart attack and
who is scheduled to leave Saigon to here-to Tripler Hospital in
Hawaii today. We both slept good that night.

The next morning I was scheduled for air evac then bumped
off- then put on again. It was during this time that I corrected the
letter written to you on the previous day and mailed the letter.

Finally at 3:00PM in the afternoon I bade farewell to the
Dr. and Nurses that had been so very good to all of us...
Back to the evac story again:

The convoy of ambulances got out to TAN SON NHUT
airport at 4:00PM and the aircraft for our evac had to take an
hour to refuel-at this time it was discovered by the attending
hospital personnel that the plane was not going to come in here to
the Philippines because of a typhoon and so they had to pull all the
patients in a staging area overnight rather than return them to a
hospital. It was crowded but better than I expected-much like a
front line battalion aid station.

The wounded-the seriously wounded were placed in beds
and attended to first and I did what I could to help the corpsmen
make them as comfortable as possible at first. We were told that
we would evac early the next morning. I helped as many as I could,
feeding them or cutting meat for them. Since I was in uniform and
was wearing my rank many would wonder just what the hell a
Captain-pilot was doing walking around the ward and I would
have to explain to them I was a patient too.

I don't know how to say this to you Alice- but I felt guilty
for even being there with a full and whole body- and I still feel this
way. I am being honest with you darling- I am in a God Damned

war and I intend to survive, but the sights I have seen as a pilot-of wounded-and then last night in that shelter-men torn to shreds with tubes running into them-casts seeping blood-the faces and eyes of these kids, has infuriated and humbled me. These people knew that they were going home to the states and were not unhappy about it- yet, I saw some cry because they were worried about the squad they were leaving behind and they would call out names to see if their buddies-wounded at the same time- in the same action- were there with them. The Chief Doctor came around to me finally and asked how I felt- I told him I was weak-but more than that- I needed a drink and wanted to get over to the AF Officers Club. He told me I had earned it and rounded up two officers to accompany me over there.

The place was mobbed with pilots-some who fly a lot, some who seldom get off the ground. I sat at a table and could tell what stories were real and who had a right to be drinking. I didn't get drunk. I had about 6 Scotch and sodas over a four hour period. I sat with one AF pilot who was ready to turn in his wings because- thru no fault of his own- he had dropped ordnance on our own troops. I didn't tell him that some of those men in my ward were those he had hit-but just let him talk it out.

Then someone remembered it was HO CHI MINH's birthday and we all stood and sang:
"Happy Birthday to you, Happy Birthday to you"
"Happy Birthday HO CHI MINH, Happy Birthday-
"Fuck you!"

The end of the song heralded the smashing of glasses and the club manager declared free drinks for all. Quite a blast! I had one more drink and found my way back to the shelter where I stayed up all night talking, and lighting cigarettes and etc. for the serious cases. By the time the sun had come up- I didn't feel tired at all-and for the first time in days, felt as though I was a man again-on my feet.

We got off on time this morning and I slept most of the way over here. They weren't sure we could even make it in because of the typhoon -but here we are and tomorrow-if the typhoon permits we will be evaced to our different destinations, Mine will be Japan

at Camp Drake and the address is as follows:
RANK, NAME
SERIAL NUMBER
249TH HOSPITAL (ARMY)
APO SAN FRANSISCO 96267...

*Please Alice- do not worry yourself one small bit about me-
I am convinced (as Ruth said in her letter) that a combination of
medications has knocked my legs out from under me. The fact that
I am going to Japan is just another step in the line to check out
every possibility...*

*Just go on with your daily living and keep the home safe
and happy. Your job is the big one and you are doing it well-
believe me.*

I love you. I love our boys.
Sleep tight-sweet dreams-
Your husband- John

May 25, 1966
Camp Drake
Japan

My Darling Wife-
*This letter to you is overdue since I arrived here on the
night of the 23rd. I meant to write to you sooner but held off until I
could write at least something conclusive. Also, I was extremely
tired from the trip and have slept at every opportunity.*

*O.K. then, I get here and was admitted to the Officers Ward
while they examined my records to determine the problem. Several
doctors seemed to agree that they could not determine the reason
up here in Japan for my initial hospital entrance of chronic
exhaustion-but seem also to agree that the only reason for my
erratic walk and dizzy spells while in the 3rd Field Hospital in
Saigon was due to excessive medication (as Ruth guessed in her
last letter to me).*

*So-now-get this! They yanked me out of the Officers Ward
and have me in a ward with only two other patients- nerve cases,
and under the care of the Bug Doctor. How about that? The reason
they say-is to prove there is nothing wrong with me in the head-*

and that the medicine was the problem. The idea of being in here bugs me but the Doctor has already cleared me to return to full duty. The rub is that it takes about two weeks to process out of here and get back in the system to be returned to duty.

So, as a best guess- I will leave here around June 8 and go to Camp Zama-north of here where they due the paperwork to get a man on the airplane. Sometimes it takes a week to get out of there. God! So who knows when I'll get back to duty? Maybe around the middle or the third week of June...

Not having my mail from you hurts and I wish I knew what was going on with my family back home...

Don't worry about me Angel. I guess your not anyway-I'm O.K. My only worries are with you there at home and how all of you are doing.

I have got to sign off for now and get in the mail before pick up time.

Your loving (Nutty) husband John

Friday June 3, 1966
Camp Drake Hospital
Japan

My Darling Wife

Today has been a great day! I spent the entire morning reading all of the mail you have sent to me. The unit packaged all of my letters and sent them up here in one envelope-plus I received one letter from you-written in answer to my letter from the Philippines. So I had wonderful morning going through some of the finest letters you have written to date. And now-at last, I have something to write to you about-7 letters to answer...

O.K. Alice-here is the final outcome of this trip to the Hospital as best as I can reconstruct it for you. To begin with, I had a kidney stone and prostitus-remember? Well, when I left the 93rd they sent my medical records to D.C. instead of to my own records at the Flight Surgeons office back at the Unit.

Then I arrived back at duty with Bronchitis-which was going around the 93rd while I was there. Ok then the Dr. gives me a bunch of medications for this too-for over a week and not knowing for sure what I was given at the 93rd-only guessing. Then I complain of chronic fatigue and he admits me to the 3rd Field for a checkup in Saigon. They put me on Librium Pills-'slowdown pills'-8 capsules per day. I talk to the Bug Doctor there as a matter of a process of elimination-nothing wrong according to him. Yet the Doctor there runs out of guesswork and sends me up here with a diagnosis of Neurosemia- a disease of weak nerves. Once I get here, the Neurologist examines me and says nothing wrong. To go back a bit here, several days before I left Saigon, the doctor there took me off all the pills-after he had already processed me out to Japan. So, as I left Saigon I was feeling better and didn't have a gait to the right in my walk by the time I got to the Philippines or here in Japan.

O.K. now back to Japan. Since the Neurologist couldn't find anything wrong with me-the Bug Doctor again.

Four days of interviews-discussing past history, present job-wife-kids-the whole scheme of things (I played the game along with him). He tells me that there are 4 categories they have for Mental Diseases in the Army. No's 1 and 2 are Crazy and Nuts-No. 3 is Character Disorder- and No. 4 is "No Disease". I told him that the only thing I could accept is No. 4, you know, "Support Mental Health-or I'll kill you!"-anyway he told me quite a few things at the end of the interview. For instance-all pilots are a little bit crazy (Hell-he didn't tell me anything new there) but mainly that I was going back to duty with a diagnosis of NO DISEASE (No. 4) So I put away my switchblade.

He also told me the following items of interest.

I am a well adjusted individual-in the normal group, but with the following provisions-that I am an 'angry man' at something and probably have been for several years. I should watch out for it or it could be bad at the wrong moment.

I am an aggressive type-and often intimidate people away from me by my attitude towards people and events. Yet while I am an aggressive-0 which is good for me in war because of immediate reaction to 'loss of my own life' situations, I also am torn between going full blast in war and the other side of me which is tender and manifested in my abrupt unreal concern for my home-wife and children. He explained that not one of the two can occupy me at the same time in a crucial situation one or the other must have the whole street. He feels that he doesn't know all about me (he doesn't) and I am an interesting case-for a normal individual since he is especially interested in pilots. I'm the first one to come through his office that was trying to get back to Viet-Nam. All others were trying to get out of going back.

Hell-I'm no hero and damned sure dont want to go back and get shot at-who does? I made sure he understood that. Its just that I'm there and will have to stay there until I can come home. I have accepted that and there are no shades of gray there. Anyway-for all of this trip-I got a free bug doctor consultation and some decent chow-plus your china and Silver-and my fan.

The conclusion was-that-just as Ruth said- too many medicines to fast. Combine that with the heat and my already pooped condition and little records for them to go by initially, and that is how I got here. The doctors all said I was in top shape and very sound physically and mentally-so, do you still want me-or not?

The time this afternoon has fled by me fast and if I want to get this in the mail, I had better end it now. So I will write you again tomorrow. There is so very much I want to write about and I give most of to tomorrow to do that.

Closing for now then- remember

> *I love you   John*

> *Saturday June 4*
> *Camp Drake*
> *Japan*

Angel-

I got the letter in the mail too late yesterday so I could have just as well continued it.

Your letters that arrived were read through and through yesterday. Also, I got the letter you wrote the day I called. Your letters are all that I could expect-more even. Your easy style-and the events you relate to me are worthy of a book. Reading through them, I discover that I am missing so very much of the lives of our boys. Doug catching his first fish-I can picture it perfectly and am thankful, that, at least, I'll see a picture of it. 'The Fort' that they are building-it must be done by now- I know we will have a snap of that to- for our memories. The way you described the boys coming home from the 'Park' with their toys and the baby birds first flight fills the day in and day out emptiness that I have to accept. I wonder how I can report things to you-what do I have to say? Nothing at all, to help you ease through the days when you are lonely and the presence of our boys with you becomes a burden at times, rather than a joy. You are content there-and this is not a fib or a lie to yourself, or me. But you must have restless and doubtfull days with many more to come. I wish I could help you my darling. Yet all I can do is be on the receiving end of your letters and benefit from them.

I know you're proud of our sons Alice- and your love for them is growing more with each day that you share their lives. These things like Mark helping in the morning-and Doug sleeping with you. Yet still your being both Mother and Father when you help catch a frog or- are the one they have to run and shout "Snake" to. Will it be ever more lonely for you when Mark starts kindergarten? I suspect that it will be- and you will have more time yet to be alone-and feel lonely.

Alice-these are the big reasons I'm going to get out of the Army. Once upon a time I wanted to fly and be free as a bird and tied not to one thing or one person. But before I could realize my hopes, a gal came along and changed my whole life for the better and our children arrived and in a few short years, my values changed-and I grew up to them.

Flying and war are all very masculine and all that and I am sure that without all of you in my lives-I would be a hell-fire type man all set to go to the limit in my involvement in this war. But the three best things that ever happened to me-are you and my boys and I have them and you foremost in my life now. And I am better for it.

What kind of man would I be to run off every other year to leave with the responsibility of the boys and your own lives alone? I wouldn't be what I consider a real man is. So its for you above all

Alice, that I am going to leave the service. I just can't pat you on the cheek, tell you your doing a good job and "I'll see you in a year."-once every other year.

Dont apologize for letting off steam- or feel in any way sorry that you have let me know how hard your job is. I dont really know. I can only imagine-and that is enough for me. Please believe that I appreciate the weight of it on you and since it is our lives that want to maintain, I can see no other way than to do it together. If I am less a man in your eyes by thinking this way- then so be it. I dont need to smell my own sweat, the elation of fear and live in a uniform to think of myself as a man. I hope that I dont drop in your esteem in some way by becoming more domesticated in my approach to my responsibilities.

I asked the doctor a personal question that has been bothering me- I haven't had hardly any sexual desire lately and was beginning to worry about it. He says its probably all of the medications I've had, plus my mind has just put it out of the picture for me. I was concerned because I'm going to have to do some good performing for two weeks in Hawaii.

Hell, like I said- I was worried but I guess my fears were groundless because two of your letters touched on 'us' briefly and all I had to do was just read your words and I felt the old stirring inside of me and yearned for you so badly that it hurt like a low stomach ache.

The letter I got last night-was the first one where you have come out and said that you missed my body and my loving. Just thinking about it now has made me excited- and no I dont think I'll have any problem when the time comes.

Take good care of your beautiful self for us will you? Tonight when you lay in bed, reach up and cup your breasts and just think to yourself that my mouth will be there for all and whatever you want of it-soon. I treat your nipples as much as they want until the time comes to mount you. I'll take care of you my beautiful princess. Your the only woman is this whole world for me and I just dont desire any one but you. You're quite a woman.

Well Angel, I received letters (in answer to ones I wrote) from-SIS, GORVAD JACK MORRIN, SHORTY, FRADY,

RODGERS AND KEEFER. So if there ever going to get answered-maybe I should start on some of them now.

There will be so much more to write to you-I'd really like to sit down with you on the couch and just your hear voice and talk with you about all sorts of things. Just listen to talk for hours on end. I miss that too-very much. No guarantee that you wouldn't wind up undressed on the floor later on- but its all part of living with you- our things we do together-talking, loving, sharing the same bed-all those things about you I miss very much.

Believe me.   I love you John

Monday June 6
Camp Drake Japan

My Darling-

I waited until this evening to write to you...

The STARS + STRIPES has been printing a lot of stories about kidnappings, killings, rapes, families burning, fire and etc. A lot of them. These stories greatly concern me Alice and I worry about yours and the boys safety as well as out on the Freeway. Nothing I can do about it I know- but there it is anyway...

I have just been advised that I will leave here for Camp Zama on Friday the 10th for duty. I'll be there a couple of days before I get a ride on the way back to Viet-Nam. So I should be back at the unit around the 15th. As soon as I get back, I will go to work on my leave...

I cant wait to get out of this place Alice. Not everyone here is going home to the States. A lot of them are for chronic backaches and the sort-that cant be traced down-and so they ship them home. The thought depresses me and so I'd just as soon get out of here and back to that hole in Viet-Nam. At least there- I can start the wheels rolling on my leave and follow through on it.

As I said earlier darling- I worry a great deal about all of you there. Please take good care-lock all the doors and etc.

I love all of you very much. Stay sweet, safe, and mine

John

Thursday, June 9
Camp Drake, Japan

Princess-

I had quite a day yesterday...
I caught a sedan over to Tachikawa AB
It was ever better than 1962 when I was there on my way home
from Korea...

I walked around the 'Shopper's Mart' for about 2 hours
trying to figure out just exactly what to buy on my limited funds,
figuring in the cost of packing and postage.. Lord, I wish you could
have seen it!-Lamps, hairshades, jewelry, silks, woodcarvings,
stoneware, silver coffee sets (gold too)-and thousands of paintings
and beautiful woodblock prints. All of this stuff at 1/4 the cost in
the States.

Finally, I zeroed in on the paintings to start with. Now
Alice, I feel that in our furnishings we already lean heavily toward
the Orient-and so I wanted something for us that would be quiet
and subtle and yet be outstanding. So I went for the woodstock
prints...then I went to the woodcarvings: I bought you a sitting
Bhudda...I did get you a bracelet of "adventurine" Jade (imitation
Jade) and a silver chain necklace with jade pendant on it...my one
big regret is -that here was absolutely nothing to send our boys-
NOTHING. I hope when all this stuff arrives, that our boys will
understand this-and forgive me. I can't tell you, how bad I feel
about this. If I could just find something-anything. But I cant...both
should take 3-4 weeks to get to you...

Hell, Im in good shape compared to these other characters
in here. These other officers have blown entire bank accounts and
haven't got a thing to show for it but a big head each morning. Bed
+ Booze must cost a fortune in downtown Tokyo...

Remember-" Its a Mad, Mad, World?" Well, last night I
saw one that will tickle the kids to no end. Its called the 'Great
Race'-Jack Lemmon. I think Doug, Mark, and you will enjoy it
even more. If you get the chance, take them to see it. I thought
about all of you laughing with me all the way through the movie
and could just imagine Doug getting a fit of laughter that wouldn't
stop. Try to see it with them.

*After the movie got out I walked back to the ward and layed
down and swore-for an hour about not having more money on me
to buy all the things I wanted for you. I finally went to sleep and
woke up in the morning feeling very much like a man. To be
truthfull, I was hard for over an hour, laying with my eyes closed
and thinking about nothing in this world-but you. You were very
real and close and I can remember every detail of and about you.*

Its hell, but its nice, soft and warm hell at least.

Who's my Princess?

John

Saturday June 11
Camp Zama, Japan

Angel-

My last day in Japan...

*I took my medical records down to the local Flight Surgeon
and had him take a look at the Clinical Evaluation sheet remarks.
Quite interesting. He read through the remarks and said I have the
cleanest bill of health he's ever seen from a Bug Doctor. He then
included his own remarks that tied the knot-he concluded, on
paper, that excessive medications were the whole problem. End of
chapter...*

*So when all the packages get to you-china, silver,
paintings, and other stuff-about $200 dollars worth of goodies
counting the fan I bought myself.*

*I would go easy on showing the small gifts around Ruth,
Sis+Carol if I were you Alice. I wanted to get them some jewelry
but had no dough. Thats hard to explain, so soft pedal it there will
you?*

*Still nothing for the kids-or Carols kids-or Cynthia.
Nothing but junk-so nothing at all...*

*Camp Zama is a quiet and pretty place-and outside my
BOQ window are endless Japanese fir and evergreen trees If I
wasnt in such a rush to get back to that hell hole where I can once
again read your letters to me, I would like to stay on here. Yet May
and June are bad months in Tokyo because of the rain and it
somehow seems gloomy. So I had best get on that 707 and be back*

at TAN SON NHUT at Midnight. Thank God I got a jet-Pan Am no less. So my next letter to you will be from back at the old grind again.

I love you princess and have missed you-and my boys so very, very much these last few gloomy days. Sleep tight and sleep well tonight-all of you

Love John

My Darling Wife-   *June 12 1966*
Phu Loi

I arrived back in Viet Nam at 6:00AM this morning after an all night flight that started at midnite on a new 727. We stopped for an hour in Taipei, Formosa. I didnt sleep on the trip and have yet to get to sleep- I guess I'm wound up being tired any more today...

I read with amusement about Doug's new bike and about Mark trying to learn to ride Doug's. Sure honey, I agree with your decision about a bike for Doug and with the summer vacation coming on he will have a wonderful time with it. Just think, Mark will be riding a bike before he even starts kindergarten!

I'm going to sign off for now honey and take a shower and go to bed. I'm tireder than I thought.

June 13,1966
Phu Loi

Angel-

I woke up tired from sleeping so hard. I sure feel great today even though I'm back in this damned heat again. I guess a large part of it is because I'm back where I can get my mail-look at the pictures you send. . .

I learned from my Korea experience what I should have bought you and me and have now done just about all I wanted to do. One regret: I could have bought you a Fur Coat in Japan for about $500- worth about $1500 back in the States.

Now about our trip. I'm going to make every effort to get to Hawaii- but if I cant a round trip for military standby costs about $600 dollars. If I only use it one way, it will cost about $400.00.

I learned that while Hawaii is back on the R & R list-leaves still haven't been approved yet by Westmoreland-seems as though they will but its just a matter of time. So I will plug away at it...

I've made up my mind for sure- I want you Brunette-not blonde. Is that alright or am I asking something unreasonable?

Because I love you   John

June 14, 1966
Phu Loi

Angel-

I went down to Saigon today to get the pay I missed by not being here and my next months $150 early. Just missed being in the middle of a Bhuddist riot downtown. Sorry "Bout That-I'm all for killing off all the God Damned Catholics and Bhuddists too. When we do that, there wont be any people over here left to defend and we can all go home.

I got back to the unit-no mail from you so I figure you had a busy weekend for yourself. I'm looking for some mail tomorrow.

While in Saigon I found out the following:

(1) A determination will come out soon on Hawaii. Army has given the go on it MACV is holding up for some reason. I have a Sergeant down there looking into it for me and he will advise me as soon as he finds out something.

(2) I received an answer to a letter I wrote to Frady. He asked about when I can get R & R and for leave and wanted to know if you could come over and meet me in Bankok. If Hawaii gives us too much trouble, this might not be a bad idea since I could go there and back free with no trouble at all. Or could do the same to Hong Kong-but believe me, come August, with the one year rotation of troops happening then and new troops replacing them, space available from to and from Hawaii is going to be nil and we can almost depend on me paying the Military Standby Rate...

Frady says that we could be guests of Air America and their is a beach south of Bankok where swimming, water skiing and the such goes on...

Well- we had our first death in the company a few days ago, not from hostile fire though. We've had some enlisted men evaced to the States with wounds but no deaths from enemy action. Remember that news article I sent you about Black Virgin Mountain? Two of our Majors were landing at the top with an internal load of gas drums on board and fell through short and rolled over. The crew chief was burned completely along with a passenger-2 dead. How the rest of the crew got out at all is a mystery to all. The ship was a fireball and rolled into a village and killed 19 civilians and VN soldiers.

We had another ship shot down today-they recovered it before nightfall-no one hurt. Must be about 7 or 8 shot down so far now-all recovered though. A lousy war.

It rained today and now it is hot and muggy as the devil and the bugs are out in full force and driving us nuts-me especially, so I am going to sign off for now-and wish you.

Sweet dreams   John

June 15, 1966

DEAR DOUG
HI! HOW ARE YOU DOUG? I HOPE YOU ARE WELL AND
HAVING A NICE TIME. MOMMY WROTE TO ME THAT SHE
BOUGHT YOU AND MARK A TETHER BALL. THAT IS NICE. I
HOPE YOU HAVE FUN PLAYING WITH IT WITH MARK AND
YOUR FRIENDS. REMEMBER MARK IS NOT AS TALL AS YOU
YOU AND GIVE HIM A CHANCE TO HIT IT AND YOU BOTH
WILL HAVE LOTS OF FUN AS TWO BROTHERS SHOULD
HAVE FUN TOGETHER. REMEMBER TO BE CAREFULL ON
HOW HARD YOU HIT IT TOWARDS MARK. I GOT A BLOODY
NOSE FROM A THETHER BALL HITTING ME IN THE FACE
WHEN I WAS A SMALL BOY. I DONT WANT MY BOYS HURT
LIKE THAT.
    MOMMY ALSO WROTE TO ME THAT YOU DID VERY
WELL IN SCHOOL AGAIN THIS YEAR. I AM PROUD OF YOU

*AND YOU SHOULD BE PROUD OF YOURSELF. YOU ARE A
SMART BOY.*

*SO YOU HAVE A NEW STINGRAY BIKE! BOY, I BET
YOU LIKE IT. YOUR FIRST BIKE IS A GOOD ONE TOO. I
HOPE MARK LIKES IT AND WILL HAVE FUN ON IT. WHEN
MARK LEARNS HOW TO RIDE, THINK OF ALL THE FUN YOU
TWO GUYS WILL HAVE!*

*MOMMY SENT ME PICTURES OF YOU TWO BOYS AND
YOU TWO SURE LOOK HAPPY AND HEALTHY. YOU TWO
LOOK LIKE YOU HAVE GROWN TALLER SINCE I LEFT.*

*ARE YOU REMEMBERING TO BE NICE TO MOMMY
AND HELP HER BY BEING GOOD TO EACH OTHER AND NOT
FIGHTING?*

*REMEMBER THAT MOMMY NEEDS YOUR HELP AND I
NEED TO BE SURE THAT YOU ARE TRYING YOUR BEST TO
HELP HER THIS WAY.*
I LOVE YOU DOUG.
BE CAREFULL
GOOD NIGHT
SWEET DREAMS
SLEEP TIGHT

Love-
DAD

June 15, 1966

DEAR MARK!
*Hi! HOW ARE YOU MARK? I HOPE YOU ARE WELL AND
HAVING A NICE TIME.*

*NOW THAT DOUG HAS A NEW BIKE, I BET YOU WILL
LEARN TO RIDE THE OTHER ONE. IT IS A REAL GOOD BIKE
AND IS NICE.*

*DO YOU STILL DRIVE YOUR "T-BIRD" CAR?
THAT IS THE BEST LITTLE CAR IN THE WHOLE WIDE
WORLD AND I NEVER SAW A BOY DRIVE A CAR BETTER
THAN YOU.*

*HOW DO YOU LIKE SUNDAY SCHOOL? IS IT FUN? DO
YOU SING SONGS AND PLAY GAMES? YOU MUST LOOK*

*NICE IN YOUR SUNDAY SCHOOL CLOTHES AND MOMMY
MUST BE PROUD OF YOU IF YOU LOOK NICE.*

*NOW THAT SUMMER IS HERE, DOUG IS OUT OF
SCHOOL AND I BET YOU TWO BOYS WILL HAVE LOTS OF
FUN TOGETHER AS TWO BROTHERS SHOULD.*

*JUST THINK MARK, AFTER SUMMER IS OVER, YOU
WILL BE STARTING TO GO TO KINDERGARTEN SCHOOL.*

*THE SAME SCHOOL THAT DOUG GOES TO EACH
DAY. YOU CAN RIDE ON THE BUS TO SCHOOL WITH MANY
OTHER KIDS.*

*YOU CAN PLAY GAMES WITH ALL THE OTHER
CHILDREN AND MAKE LOTS OF NEW FRIENDS AND LEARN
MANY THINGS TOO.*

*YOUR BROTHER DOUG, HAS DONE VERY WELL IN
SCHOOL AND I KNOW YOU WILL HAVE FUN AND DO WELL
TOO BECAUSE YOU ARE SO SMART. I AM PROUD OF YOU.*

*ARE YOU HELPING MOMMY BY TRYING YOUR BEST
TO BE GOOD ALL OF THE TIME? I HOPE SO.*
I LOVE YOU MARK
BE CAREFULL
GOOD NIGHT
SWEET DREAMS
SLEEP TIGHT

Love-
DAD

June 16, 1966
Phu Loi

Darling-

Another day with no mail from you...

*I wrote my two boys- a letter each, last night. It was way
over due to both of my precious sons and I enjoyed sending them
each a letter. I tried to imagine the mail arriving there are the boys
each opening their letters, and then Doug patiently reading each
one out loud. I was very homesick for them last night.*

Tomorrow I begin flying again.

I hear something unusual yesterday. Two of the Battalion Staff Officers went to Hawaii while it was restricted. They were able to do this because they had already bought their tickets and had set aside funds and so were allowed to go. Yet I heard that(while I was in the hospital) they returned and were very gloomy and changed men meeting-meeting their wives seemed to be the reason. They have shipped out to other units now- or I would talk to them. I can only guess at what made them cranky and hard to get along with after they came back and cant imagine myself acting the same way...

There is nothing about this war or country, or the people, that interest me so my life over here is dull and without any gleam in it...

Nothing else to write about tonight. It is raining hard outside to even walk around among the tents- not that there is anything new there anyway.   *Love   John*

June 18 1966

Angel-

I received two letters. One yesterday, and one today. One you wrote on the 9th and one on the 12th. So the mail delivery fouled up somewhere...

I got four hours flying time yesterday-after laying off for over 45 days. It was much different than flying on "Birmingham." No dust or grime in the cockpit and it is a little cooler now with a heavy cloud cover over the ground most of the time. During the monsoon, about 8/10 of the ground is covered at all times by low hanging clouds. It makes flying a lot harder since it is quite easy to get lost yet it remains 10 degrees cooler on the ground. It rains everyday in the afternoon and once at night usually. While the water drainage is a little better now-everything is pretty muddy and nothing ever really dries. The odor of mold is on all of my clothes and my boots are green around the soles since I was gone for so long and my wall locker closed up with no air getting into it...

I'll be anxious to read your next letter to find out how my boys are. Take care of all you-please.

I love all you   John

June 20 1966

Princess-

Another Monday-the start of another week. Not that Saturdays or Sundays are any different over here. Yesterday and today are scorchers and I am sitting on my bunk with the breeze from my fan blowing down on me. I mounted the fan to the side of my wall locker which is at the foot of my bed. That way I have a breeze across me at night even though its effect is reduced by the mosquito net. So I'm quite comfortable right now here on my foam rubber mattress, drinking a Dad's Old Fashion Root Beer(on ice) and looking forward to quitting time when I mix myself a Hawaiian Mai Tai (Rum Drink) or have a Kahlua' on-the-rocks, or a Vodka or Gin Gimlet. As a matter of fact, the only thing that could make me move right now would be a mortar attack-and then I wouldn't have to move far to the sandbags, being sure to take my drink with me, of course.

Another thing nice about my situation is the outdoor movies which are shown not far away from our tent. The movie last night was "Goldfinger"- which I think you saw with me in Alaska. No matter what the movie there is always some crucial scene in it-you know, where the gal is getting ready for the showers and etc. Anyway the projector is shot to hell and the film will run along fine until one of these scenes comes along and then, sure as anything, the film starts jumping and they have to shut down, start again and the process repeats itself over and over while around one hundred people curse the projectionist. Or the Air Force will fly over head and drop flares around the outer perimeter and light up the sky so bright that we cannot see the scene. A hardship tour indeed...

I received a letter from Hawaii. We have reservations in one of the apartments 8-15 August....

Now- this-we have a new unit and battalion designation and it goes on our mail. So read my return address carefully for this new glory-type address. This is what happens when we get too many Colonels and Generals over here that want to command tough sounding units. Oh well, something else for their troubles.

Not much else to write about today- so I will get this in the mail even though it too late to get it out today.

Sweet Dreams John

June 21, 1966

Darling Alice-

I got up at 0530 today for a mission that was fouled up from the start-and it ended before it even got started. A million mix-ups led to it and I was pulled off after 2:00 hours to stand by for the IG inspection, which the motor pool passed with flying colors. Today was another scorcher, I dont even know what the temp reading was, but it was an extension of hell. The monsoon is getting started in earnest now and rain, once a day is a sure thing. It looks as though we will get ours again tonight-just in time to rain out the movie which is the only diversion there is and the only graphic contact with the outside world-other than letters and pictures from home.

After lunch today, I laid down on my steel cot with the fan blowing hot air on me. If either one of my wall lockers are open, I can look up at a picture of you.

I have the family portrait on the outside of the left door, so, if that is open, I see you and the boys along with me.

Yet, if that is closed and right door is open, I see my two pin-ups of you which are inside of my right door. So either way, I cant lose...

I received my Fathers Day cards today and will stick them up on my locker tomorrow. I liked both of them very much and looked at these for quite a while.

No honey-you dont have to send me any goodies in the mail. A lot of people get stuff sent to them and a lot of it goes to waste because the heat just knocks appetites for anything sweet. But thank you Angel...

Sure wish we were sleeping side by side and huddled close

Love you
John

June 24 1966
Phu Loi

Angel-

I'll tell you the truth. I know now how we won WWII. We gathered all our Battle Plans, Secrets and etc. and dropped them on Berlin and Tokyo like leaflets. They gathered them all up, read them, believed, and acted accordingly. Being that confused by our plans-which we never follow anyway, we naturally had to win.

Logan and I flew together yesterday and hauled drums of diesel and pods of JP-4 to burn captured rice with. This was for the 1st INF. DIV naturally and they are without a doubt the most fouled up unit in the history of war.

Well you might remember John Logan's temper in Flight School. It hasn't changed and my ears were ringing after a day of hearing him expound on things. The Chaplain and Flight Surgeon went along as passengers and both had headsets on and heard both of us spew out our dissatisfaction about things. I wont bore you with details that you wouldn't understand anyway. Just to tell you that both sad and humorous.

Two Huey units of this battalion here at Phu Loi have received the sad word: to move. One to Cu Chi- the other to the Delta south of Saigon. Both have been here since November and have worked hard setting up their areas, just now finishing semi-permanent BOQ's and etc. Our sister unit, the 147th down at Vuang Tau is going to move up here and so both Chinook units will be moving into new quarters since we will move into one of the vacant areas. Not bad for us.

Our Mama-San didnt show up today and I just heard that she was arrested as a possible VC spy. How about that? Nothing would surprise me anymore. Most of us are half-sick most of the time with the 'runs', making about five trips per day to the latrine. Not so bad when you on the ground, not flying. But the cramps can really get bad up in the air. The only cure is either to get out of here (cant), stop eating (almost, since the chow is rotten)-or drink a lot of booze (we do).

The movie last night was new, but lousy and as I walked away from it to the tent, I slid in the mud and tore up my left knee cap on a rock-plus rammed a hunk of wood under my large toenail, so I'm limping around all bandaged up today.

I have resumed writing this after supper. I knocked off late this morning, figuring I'd have something to write about if the mail which comes in at noon, had a letter from you in it. It didn't.

The electricity was of all day and just came on now- so my fan is working and I am in its breeze.

The Air Force jets are striking some target just north of the field, so I imagine our artillery will be going full blast tonight and there will be little sleep at all.

Speaking of Air Force, did you ever join McLellan AFB Officers Club or the OWC or whatever it was. If so you havent mentioned it. The AF is a sore subject around here. Their ships have wiped out a couple of helicopters in landing on forward strips and the Army ends up being blamed.
I'm sick and tired of being sick and tired.

Love   John

June 25 1966
Phu Loi

Angel-
I came in from flying with Logan again and had two letters and box awaiting me in my pidgeon hole. I opened the box first and ate some of my cookies while I read your two letters. The thought of the cookies and the badge and your accompanying note got to me and I couldn't stop the tears as I thought of all of you. Thank you darling-and thank my boys for me, for their thoughtfulness. I will have my pictures taken with my badge and send Doug a print.

There was a party in the tent next door last night- a farewell blast for Major Keaton who leaves for Vuang Tau to take over the 147th. Every one there got pretty drunk and it lasted until the wee hours. I was there too and spent most of my time talking with Logan who was more tired than drunk. I wound up breaking up a fight between him and some thug from battalion and then I got with in it with Maj. Monroe *%$#&@&%$#@#$%&&* . I was fed up with his damned mouth and attitude and up laying one on his jaw-so it was over before it started. He was long overdue.

Tonight, things are pretty quiet around the area, everyone is staying in their own tent and resting. There is a big storm brewing up and we will be in a deluge soon. Anyway, I am content here in my chair-writing to you and munching on my cookies. They ARE good.

You wrote that National Geographic had just begun to arrive. They sure took their time about it. Have you received that "Great Bands" record album yet-or have you sent for it?

Princess-I know you want to Frost your hair again but I look at your pictures all the time and harbour the thought that you-your hair will be the same when I see you again and that is why I asked you not to change your hair. You can do what you want though.

You mentioned loosing weight and that it was nerves. Oh Alice, I wish to God that you were in my arms right now. You have such a perfect little body and even if you were plump, you would look well. I know you are under a strain princess and I am still convinced you have the toughest job to do. You do it well too (the claim for furniture damage-as an example) I want you to know that I know and appreciate your situation and there is not a day or night that passes that I don't worry about you and dwell upon your situation. I've had a few nightmares about accidents at home-the boys falling in some ditch or reservoir-and the like. Its hard enough to get to sleep in this heat-and then an occasional bad dream comes along to make a long night of staring at the mosquito net in the dark- a night of all sorts of worries.

I want very much to hold you and love you this night. I wish that you and I were on the couch together and I could cradle you in one arm while I stroked your hair around your face and kissed you neck and throat. It would be a thrill for me to lay you on the floor and have you there, but if I did nothing more than just held you in my arms and listened to you purr and comforted you quietly, I would be satisfied, knowing that you were warm, soft and safe in my arms, without a worry or a care. If I am needed by you you-and needed by my sons to tuck them in at night with a story after I have helped you with the dishes and the table. Then I will continue to consider myself a rich man to be envied by all.

I need you too Alice. For that feeling of pride and respect when I look at you and watch you move amongst your family and belongings. The children and each place we have lived are such an extension of you and your mark is on all of us and all of our things. I need you to make me feel like a man-complete just as you need me to feel completely female.

Holding you in my arms softly, or thrusting myself into your body-either way, and each way with its own proper time and cause and feeling. I need you for the thrill and the glow that you make me believe is there in you because of me.

That is what I want most this night and so many other nights.

I love you, probably more than is good for me yet not as much as I will several years from now-and many years from now. You are a flower all of my own and I will care for you forever.

I'm far away- but tonight I am not lonely because you are as close to me as my heartbeat

Sleep long and sweet   John